C0-DYE-811

Adventures and Sufferings

The American Indian Captivity Narrative Through the Centuries

SPENCER TIED FOR THE NIGHT.

Adventures and Sufferings

The American Indian Captivity Narrative Through the Centuries

*An Exhibition of Books in the Collections of
The St. Louis Mercantile Library Association;
newly presented by the St. Louis Mercantile Library
at the University of Missouri – St. Louis*

by John Neal Hoover

A Catalogue and Checklist for an Exhibition
December 1, 2002 through January 15, 2003

2nd Edition, Revised
2002

Front Cover: See Items: (clockwise from upper left) 129, 1, 13, 140

Back Cover: See Items: (clockwise from upper left) 129, 12, 1, Engraving by Felix Darley, CA. 1869, "An Indian Foray in the West"

Frontispiece: see item 4

Half title vignette: *The History, Manners and Customs of the North American Indians* (Philadelphia: American Sunday School Union, n.d. (ca.1845).

Title page and colophon vignette: see item 26. Vignette on pages 41 and 75: see item 27 *(News from New England)*

Headings: see item 7

ISBN: 0-9639804-4-0, paperback; 0-9639804-5-9, Hard Cover Limited Edition

Library of Congress Control No.: 2002116665

© Copyright 1988, The St. Louis Mercantile Library Association; 2nd edition, revised with digital versions for the St. Louis Mercantile Library and The Woodcock Foundation for the Appreciation of the Arts' virtual websites, Copyright 2002; by the St. Louis Mercantile Library at the University of Missouri – St. Louis and the Board of Curators of the University of Missouri

Adventures and Sufferings
The American Indian Captivity Narrative Through the Centuries

Introduction: America's Oldest Literature, and a Centuries' Long Folk Memory

In the early part of this century, William L.R. Gifford, Head Librarian of the St. Louis Mercantile Library (indeed, the man who held the post longer than anyone in the institution's long history) attached a note to a duplicate copy of James DeShield's *Cynthia Ann Parker; the Story of Her Capture,* which the Library had recently bought: "To be kept in reserve and used if needed, particularly in case of accident to our other copy." As if to justify such an extravagance, Gifford continued: "The cost price ($8.50) is a low one, as all Indian captivity books are increasing in value." It is evident that Gifford was understating the case. Most private collectors and research institutions have seen this romantic field of Americana grow in monetary value as well as in other gauges of bibliographical desirability almost geometrically in the last few generations.

Perhaps the reason for this heightened interest is that the Indian captivity narrative, in all its many printed manifestations, is paradoxically almost as broad a genre as the early literature of the American Indian. The fascination with the field is manifold. A strong case can be made that the Indian captivity narrative is America's oldest literary type. The best narratives follow rigid stylistic conventions within which the telling, and the retelling, the subtle twists of descriptions and setting, while necessarily crucial to overall mood, are still subordinate to the narrator's emotions, tone, and veracity. Not a few narratives print emblematically on their title pages, "Truth is stranger than fiction."

These accounts have a timelessness about them. The earliest are as old as the discovery of America itself, dating at least from the account put down by the Spanish Cabeza de Vaca or Bressani in New France. By the 1600's the stories start in an ever quickening pace to follow the events of the English settlers' association with one tribe or another, from King Philip's War in the Mathers' New England, to the pressures put on the colonists by the French and Indian War. The long struggles continued into the Northwest Territory and Old Southwest, from St. Clair's Defeat, in which hundreds of soldiers were killed, being a quite serious strategic disaster, to "mop-up" affairs such as the Black Hawk War, or the Indian campaigns of Andrew Jackson. These later confrontations coincided with a marked growth in creative writing in the early Republic. They exist romantically stage center in the pages of would-be poets and writers of ballads and epics, as much or even more, if possible, than they did in real life.

Over the long centuries of the American frontier, as each documented battle, uprising, or war was spawned from across the Atlantic in the process of trying to win the American continent, a flood of brief, humble narratives of the capture of actual people held the horrified attention of an international readership for a moment, a decade, or a generation. If a narrative of a recent raid could not be had soon enough in print, so much convention had come down by the later eighteenth century that the story could be easily embroidered. That is why some accounts of captivity grew larger than life, or existed side-by-side with an actual prosaic deposition made by a "redeemed" captive, one lucky enough to make such a relation of his or her adventure. It is interesting to note that the publishers of captivity narratives unwilling to get the true facts cheated themselves and their readers. The real works, the poignant sufferings of true participants, the victims on both sides of European and American native cultural misunderstanding, revenge, retaliation and war, almost always made better reading than ersatz embellishment.

The Indian captivity narrative allowed early Americans a chance to speak for themselves in a very significant way. We learn from these early soldiers and settlers the genealogies of entire families from New Hampshire to Illinois to Arizona. We can discern what it must have been like to have lived on the frontier, at the edge of the forest or wild prairie, at the foot of the forbidding mountains, supported only by one's unchangeable faith in the inevitability of the growth of civilization. Indian customs from a multitude of tribes and separate cultures were for the first time observed and put down on paper by captives who came back to the settlements. The lone Jesuit missionary in the Mississippi Valley or on Lake Huron in the 1600's, or captured farmers in New York or Ohio were the first North American ethnologists and anthropologists.

The vivid stories profoundly influenced American art, particularly that of such nineteenth century painters as Carl Wimar, Charles Deas and George Caleb Bingham. The crude illustrations in the captivity books often became in oil or watercolor icons for the themes of the winning of the frontier by the whites-and conversely, the loss of it by the Indians. Although many great figures in American literature tried their hands at reworking an original captivity narrative, as Cotton Mather, Thoreau or Whittier reworked the story of Hannah Duston, it is most often the plain, simple prose of the common settlers, putting their thoughts and reactions down on what must have been the most nightmarish of experiences, which creates the best writings, the most compelling to modern readers. Thus, it is no accident that American literary history can be said to begin with the account wonderfully put to paper by the Puritan woman, Mary Rowlandson.

To most men and women living on the frontier at any time in American history, to be made a captive by Indians, to lose a loved one to the tomahawk or the stake, indeed to lose one's own life in the ferocity of the Indian Wars, was a rather remote possibility. The tide of settlement pushed the Indians inexorably from their birthright. Nevertheless, the narratives represent occurrences which were common enough to have passed down to us not only in separately printed pamphlets and books by the scores, but in hundreds and even thousands of newspaper and journal accounts, in compilations, local and regional histories, and anthologies which continued to be produced well after the beginning of the twentieth century. To this day such narratives manage to be reprinted. They have become as well the subject matter for dozens of motion pictures and television scripts.

The St. Louis Mercantile Library has been an avid collector of these narratives almost since its beginnings. In fact, one of the early scholars in the field was Horace Kephart, Head Librarian of the Mercantile from 1890 to 1904. Kephart built the captivity narrative collection and the general collections on the history of the American Indian into an extremely strong body of research material. He used this collection in his own edition of such classic accounts, *Captives Among the Indians* (1915). It was left to Gifford, buying from such scholarly bookselling firms as that of William Harvey Miner in St. Louis, to round out these collections. But even long before Kephart, much captivity lore came to the Library. John Dyer, Librarian here in the 1860's and 1870's, for example, bought heavily in a succession of Americana book auctions-most notably at the sale in New York in 1876 of noted ethnologist E. George Squier's personal library.

The following selective checklist is meant to show some of the strengths of the collection, and how it has grown since the first edition of *Adventures and Sufferings* in 1988 and especially to call attention to some lesser known titles which have captivity narrative content. It accompanies a new exhibition which has brought together briefly once again one of the most romantic of all forms of Americana physically, and virtually, on the Mercantile Library and the Woodcock Foundation for the Appreciation of the Arts' websites. Both sites continue to highlight American studies and art. As usual, many people were responsible for making this exhibition possible. Robert Behra, former Mercantile Library Cataloguer, deserves particular thanks in verifying authors' names and in solving a myriad of fine points concerning the earlier edition of this catalogue. Likewise, Sidney F. Huttner, formerly Curator, Special Collections at The University of Tulsa's McFarlin Library and now at the University of Iowa, was kind to offer his help and advice. Perhaps most of the credit goes, however, to a series of Librarians here at the Mercantile in the early part of this century who brought this collection together for us, and to such later ones as Clarence Miller, Elizabeth Kirchner, and Charles Bryan who ensured its preservation for future generations of scholars. Thanks should be extended as well for the new edition and its associated digital formats to Christopher Dames of the Reference staff of the University of Missouri – St. Louis Libraries; James P. Rhodes, Manuscript Curator of the

St. Louis Mercantile Library, Mary Beth Brown, and Lisa Mosby, Graduate Research Assistantship holders at the Mercantile, and as always, Jerry Maschan and Chelmsford Printing.

Today, thanks to the affiliation between the University of Missouri – St. Louis and the St. Louis Mercantile Library Association, more scholarly use of the collections has been made in the past five years than in the previous five generations of the Library's history and the institution's potential as a research center is becoming increasingly realized. Thus, it is with pleasure that we could time the reprinting of one of the Mercantile's most successful past catalogues to the use of the Indian captivity collections in a special, ongoing readings seminar (History 403) organized by the University of Missouri – St. Louis history department and the Mercantile, and I wish to dedicate this new edition to the group of graduate students who studied Indian captivity literature this fall in my class, and who read and interpreted this age-old prose through the eyes and emotions of a new century – one in which the old tales seem to have added relevance for the cultural and human truths and insight they impart to the reader.

John Neal Hoover
Executive Director
St. Louis Mercantile Library at the
University of Missouri – St. Louis
November 7, 2002

THE
INDIAN CAPTIVE;
OR A
NARRATIVE
OF THE
Captivity and Sufferings
OF
ZADOCK STEELE.

RELATED BY HIMSELF.

TO WHICH IS PREFIXED AN ACCOUNT

OF THE

BURNING OF ROYALTON.

Hath this been in your days, or even in the days of your fathers? Tell ye your children of it, and let your children tell their chidren, and THEIR children another generation.
JOEL.

MONTPELIER, Vt.
PUBLISHED BY THE AUTHOR.
E. P. WALTON, Printer.

Item 71

Adventures and Sufferings

Caroline Harris
History of the Captivity and Providential Release There from of Mrs. Caroline Harris. New York: Perry and Cooke, 1838.

" . . . who, with Mrs. Clarissa Plummer . . . were, in the Spring of 1835 . . . taken prisoners by the Camanche tribe of Indians, while emigrating from said Franklin County (N. Y.) to Texas; and after having been made to witness the tragical deaths of their husbands, and held nearly two years in bondage, were providentially redeemed there from by two of their countrymen attached to a company of Santa Fe Fur Traders."

Robert A. Sherrard
A Narrative of the Wonderful Escape and Dreadful Sufferings of Colonel James Paul. Cincinnati: Spiller, 1869. Printed for J. Drake.

" . . . after the defeat of Col. Crawford, when that unfortunate commander, and many of his men were inhumanly burnt at the stake, and others were slaughtered by other modes of torture known only to savages."

Frederic Manheim, et. al.
Affecting History of the Dreadful Distresses of Frederic Manheim's Family. Philadelphia: Printed (for Mathew Carey) by D. Humphreys, 1794.

"To which are added, the Sufferings of John Corbly's Family; An Encounter Between a White Man and Two Savages; Extraordinary Bravery of a Woman; Adventures of Capt. Isaac Stewart; Deposition of Massey Herbeson; Adventures and Sufferings of Peter Wilkinson; Remarkable Adventures of Jackson Johonnot; Account of the Destruction of the Settlements at Wyoming." The first edition of this collection of "histories" made either by deposition or by "information of persons of unexceptionable credibility" was published in Exeter in 1793. This copy lacks the frontispiece by Maverick.

4

O. M. Spencer
Indian Captivity: A True Narrative of the Capture of Rev. O.M. Spencer, by the Indians, in the Neighbourhood of Cincinnati. New York: Carleton & Porter, 1834.

5

John D. Hunter
Memoirs of a Captivity Among the Indians of North America, From Childhood to the Age of Nineteen, With Anecdotes Descriptive of Their Manners and Customs, to which is Added, Some Account of the Soil, Climate, and Vegetable Productions of the Territory Westward of the Mississippi. London: Longman, Hurst, Rees, Orme, Brown, and Green, 1824.

A celebrity in America for a brief moment, Hunter, on publication of his book, was bitterly attacked by Lewis Cass and such notable St. Louisans as William Clark, and Pierre Chouteau. See *North American Review,* Jan. 1826, pp. 94-108. Horace Kephart of the Mercantile Library even went so far as to brand the book "a rank fabrication" several generations later, so strongly was he involved in the historiography of the captivity narrative genre. Hunter was murdered in Texas shortly after his initial attempts to create a white-red buffer state, thereby incurring the enmity of Americans such as Austin and Mexican officials alike. It should be noted that George Catlin and others much later found Hunter's descriptions quite accurate. (See Richard Drinnon's edition of Hunter, New York: 1973.) With contemporary news clippings and transcriptions of Hunter's obituary tipped in.

Adventures and Sufferings

INCIDENTS OF BORDER LIFE

Item 78

ADVENTURES AND SUFFERINGS

6 *James B. Taylor*
A Narrative of the Horrid Massacre by the Indians, of the Wife and Children of the Christian Hermit, A Resident of Missouri, with a Full Account of his Life and Sufferings, Never Before Published. St. Louis: Leander W. Whiting & Co., 1840.

". . . they now appeared in still greater numbers, almost daily in view of our little settlement: and the more to torment us they amused themselves by brandishing their tomahawks, and imitating the past groans of our dying friends whom they had taken prisoners, and on whom they had inflicted cruelties too horrible to relate."

7 *Mary Barber*
The True Narrative of the Five Years' Suffering & Perilous Adventures by Miss Barber, Wife of 'Squatting Bear,' A Celebrated Sioux Chief. Philadelphia: Barclay & Co., 1872.

"Miss Barber, a native of Massachusetts, in her religious enthusiasm, resolved to go among the Indians, as missionary, and with that purpose in view married Squatting Bear, at Washington, D.C. After five years of sufferings and stirring adventures, this beautiful young lady has just returned East, and her narrative is one of deep and entrancing interest . . . A valuable feature of this work is the Indian Receipts, given by Miss Barber, for the cure of various diseases." After years of travail in the Dakota country among her husband's tribesmen, and hardships which culminated, practically speaking, in escape from an intolerable captivity, a presumably sadder but wiser-and didactic-Miss Barber warns other young women not to take the course of a "silly girl" in wishing to reform the Indian.

Adventures and Sufferings

Annie Coleson
Miss Annie Coleson's Own Narrative of Her Captivity Among the Sioux Indians. Philadelphia: Barclay & Co., 1875.

"An interesting and remarkable account of the terrible sufferings and providential escape of this beautiful young lady."

8

John Marrant
A Narrative of the Life of John Marrant, of New York, in North America: Giving an Account of His Conversion When Only Fourteen Years of Age. Leeds: Davies and Co., 1815.

" . . . His leaving his mother's house from religious motives, wandering several days in the desert without food, and being at last taken by an Indian hunter among the Cherokees, where he was condemned to die. With an account of the conversion of the king of the Cherokees and his daughter."

9

Massy Harbison
A Narrative of the Sufferings of Massy Harbison from Indian Barbarity Giving an Account of Her captivity, the Murder of Her Two Children, Her Escape, with an Infant at Her Breast; Together with some Account of the Cruelties of the Indians, on the Allegheny River, &c., During the Years 1790, '91, '92, '93, '94. Pittsburgh: D. and M. Maclean, 1828.

As Johonnot's narrative, the Harbison account refers to the resultant confusion on the frontier after the defeat of St. Clair. See as well an earlier printing in item 3.

10

ADVENTURES AND SUFFERINGS

11 *Jackson Johonnot*
The Remarkable Adventures of Jackson Johonnot, of Massachusetts, Who Served as a Soldier in the western Army, in the Expedition Under Gen. Harmar and Gen. St. Clair, Containing an Account of His Captivity, Sufferings, and Escape from the Kickappo Indians. Greenfield, Mass.: A. Phelps, 1816.

Johonnot: "There is seldom a more difficult task undertaken by a man than the act of writing a narrative of a person's own life: – especially where the incident borders on the marvellous." See also item 3 (Manheim). "On the 4th of November, 1791, a force of Americans under General Arthur St. Clair was attacked, near the present Ohio-Indiana boundary line, by about the same number of Indians led by Blue Jacket . . . Their defeat was the most disastrous that ever has been suffered by our arms when engaged against a savage foe on anything like even terms. Out of 86 officers and about 1400 regular and militia soldiers, St. Clair lost 70 officers killed or wounded and 845 men killed, wounded, or missing. The survivors fled in panic . . . Such was 'St. Clair's defeat' . . . After this unprecedented victory, the Indians became more troublesome than ever along the frontier. No settler's home was safe, and many were destroyed in the year of terror that followed." – see Kephart, *Captives Among the Indians.*

12 *Hannah Lewis*
Narrative of the Captivity and Sufferings of Mrs. Hannah Lewis, and Her Three Children. Boston: H. Trumbull, 1817.

ADVENTURES AND SUFFERINGS

The Savages conveying Mrs. *LEWIS*, and her *THREE* CHILDREN into captivity—from whom she made her escape, with her son, on the 3d April last, 1817

Item 12

"... who were taken prisoners by the Indians, near St. Louis, on the 25th May, 1815, and among whom they experienced all the cruel treatment which savage brutality could inflict. Mrs. Lewis, and her eldest son, fortunately made their escape on the 3rd April last, leaving her two youngest children in the hands of the barbarians."

13 *Frances and Almira Hall. [Rachel (later Mrs. Munson) and Sylvia (later Mrs. Horn) Hall]*

Narrative of the Capture and Providential Escape of Misses Frances and Almira Hall. [New York?: 1833?] (copyright 1832 by William P. Edwards)

"... two respectable young women (sisters) of the ages of 16 and 18, who were taken prisoners by the savages, at a frontier settlement near the Indian Creek, in May, 1832, when fifteen of the inhabitants fell victims to the bloody tomahawk and scalping knife; among whom were the parents of the unfortunate females." With an account of the *Captivity of Philip Brigdon and of the Black Hawk War.* With Charles M. Scanlan's *Indian Massacre and Captivity of the Hall Girls; Complete History of the Massacre of Sixteen Whites on Indian Creek, Near Ottawa, Ill., and Sylvia Hall and Rachel Hall as Captives in Illinois and Wisconsin During the Black Hawk War, 1832.* Milwaukee: Reic Publishing, 1915. Photographs of the Halls in later life. Also with John Reynolds' *My Own Times.* Belleville, Ill.: 1855, for the early Illinois governor's description of the Black Hawk War and the resultant depredations on the Hall girls. – See Elmer Baldwin, *History of La Salle County, Illinois.* Chicago: Rand, McNally & Co., 1877 for lengthy statements of J.W. Hall, Mrs. Horn, and Mrs. Munson.

ADVENTURES AND SUFFERINGS

Item 13

E. House
A Narrative of the Captivity of Mrs. Horn and Her Two Children. with Mrs. Harris, by the Camanche Indians, after They had Murdered Their Husbands and Travelling Companions. St. Louis: Keemle, 1839.

14

" . . . with a brief account of the manners and customs of that nation of savages of whom so little is known."

Item 14

15 Theodore A. Babb
In the Bosom of the Comanches: A Thrilling Tale of Savage Indian Life, Massacre and Captivity Truthfully Told by a Surviving Captive. Dallas: Hargreaves, 1912.

"The closing days of the trying Indian struggles upon the frontiers of Texas." Edited by Albert Sidney Stinnett.

16 Samuel L. Metcalf
Collection of Some of the Most Interesting Narratives of Indian Warfare in the West. Lexington, Ky.: William G. Hunt, 1821.

". . . containing an account of the adventures of Colonel Daniel Boone, one of the first settlers of Kentucky, comprehending the most important occurrences relative to its early history. . . to which is added, an account of the expeditions of Genl's. Harmer, Scott, Wilkinson, St. Clair, & Wayne."

17 Joseph Persinger
The Life of Jacob Persinger. Sturgeon, Mo.: Moody & M'Michael, 1861.

". . . who was taken by the Shawnee Indians when an infant; with a short account of the Indian troubles in Missouri; and a Sketch of the adventures of the author."

From the narrative: "The squaw who adopted him had two sons. She took great pains to rear them according to Indian usage. Never expecting to give up the white child, she raised him as her own sons. Every morning she would immerse them in water, at all seasons of the year, and make them run about until they were dry, and then take them into

ADVENTURES AND SUFFERINGS

her wigwam. When they were young, during several years, she would tie boards to their backs in order that they should grow straight. She took great pains in learning them to swim, and hunt with the bow and arrows; and in a few years she gave her white son a gun. The Indians were still hostile to the whites; they told him that 'the whites were cowards and would not stand fire.'"

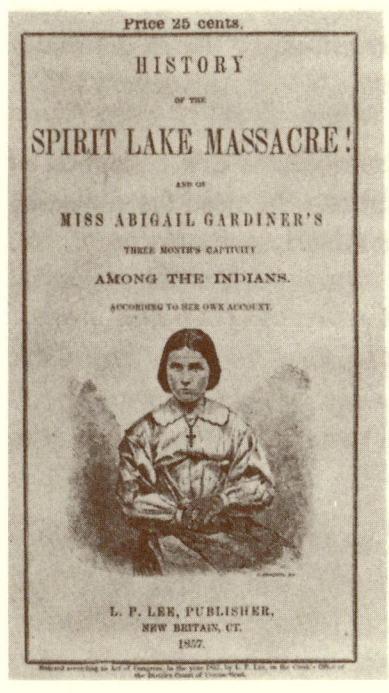

18

L. P. Lee
History of the Spirit Lake Massacre! 8th March, 1857, and of Miss Abigail Gardiner's Three Month's Captivity Among the Indians. New Britain, Ct.: Lee, 1857.

A record of Iowa Indian uprisings and the Sioux wars of the period in the region.

Item 18

ADVENTURES AND SUFFERINGS

19 *Elias Cornelius*
The Little Osage Captive, an Authentic Narrative: To Which are added Some Interesting Letters, Written by Indians. York: Alexander, 1824.

Indians took captives among each other's tribes, as this collection of such missionary accounts attests, which stresses the need for education and further religious training of the native Americans.

20 *Timothy Flint*
Biographical Memoir of Daniel Boone, The First Settler of Kentucky: Interspersed with Incidents in the Early Annals of the Country. Cincinnati: Conclin, 1842, 1846; 1856 (with title variant *The First White Man of the West,* etc.)

Flint, noted pioneer historian of the Ohio and Mississippi Valley, wrote several works with captivity narrative content, and in this vein most notably described the exploits of Boone, the prototypical frontiersman. With Flint's *Indian Wars of the West; Containing Biographical Sketches of Those Pioneers Who Headed the Western Settlers in Repelling the Attacks of the Savages, Together with a View of the Character, Manners, Monuments, and Antiquities of the Western Indians.* Cincinnati: E.H. Flint, 1833. Together with W.H. Bogart's *Daniel Boone and the Hunters of Kentucky.* Auburn: Miller, Orton & Mulligan, 1854; and a European illustration of the capture of Boone's daughter in *Jugend-Album; Blätter zur Angenehmen und Lehrreichen Unterhaltung im Häuslichen Kreise.* Stuttgart: Eduard Hallberger: "Bilder aus Daniel Boone's Leben" and John S. Jenkins" *The Lives of Patriots and Heroes.* Auburn: Derby, 1847.

Also with the French edition of John Filson's *Histoire de Kentucke, Nouvelle Colonie a l'Ouest de la Virginie.* Paris: 1785.

Adventures and Sufferings

Nelson Lee 21
Three Years Among the Camanches, the Narrative of Nelson Lee, the Texan Ranger Containing a Detailed Account of His Captivity Among the Indians. Albany: Baker Taylor, 1859.

Thomas Baldwin 22
Narrative of the Massacre, by the Savages, of the Wife and Children of Thomas Baldwin. New York: Martin and Wood, 1835.

". . . who, since the melancholy period of the destruction of his unfortunate family, has dwelt entirely alone, in a hut of his own construction, secluded from human society, in the extreme western part of the state of Kentucky."

Item 22

ADVENTURES AND SUFFERINGS

23 *R. B. Stratton*
Captivity of the Oatman Girls; Being an Interesting Narrative of Life Among the Appache and Mohave Indians. San Francisco: Whitton, Towne & Co's Excelsior Steam Power Presses, 1857.

Item 23

ADVENTURES AND SUFFERINGS

Josiah Priest — 24
A True Narrative of the Capture of David Ogden, Among the Indians, in the Time of the Revolution. Lansingburgh: W.B. Harkness, 1840.

". . . and of the slavery and sufferings he endured, with an account of his almost miraculous escape after several years' bondage."

Susannah Willard Johnson — 25
A Narrative of the Captivity of Mrs. Johnson. Windsor, Vt.: Alden Spooner, 1807.

". . . an account of her sufferings, during four years with the Indians." Taken prisoner at Charlestown, N.H., August, 29, 1754. With the Huntting Company's reprint of 1907, *A Narrative of the Captivity of Mrs. Johnson.*

John Knight, John Slover — 26
Indian Atrocities; Narratives of the Perils and Sufferings of Dr. Knight and John Slover, Among the Indians, During the Revolutionary War. Cincinnati: James, 1867.

Increase Mather — 27
A Brief History of the war with the Indians in New-England, from June 24, 1675, (when the First Englishman was Murdered by the Indians) to August 12, 1676, when Philip, alias Metacomet, the Principal Author and Beginner of the War, was Slain. London: Richard Chiswell, 1676.

ADVENTURES AND SUFFERINGS

With Samuel Penhallow's *The History of the Wars of New-England, With the Eastern Indians.* Boston: Fleet, Gerrish and Henchman, 1726 and the earliest American edition of Cotton Mather's *Magnalia Christi Americana: or the Ecclesiastical History of New England.* Hartford: Andrus, 1820 (from the London, 1702 edition) including Mather's early account of Hannah Duston. "A Notable Exploit: Dux Faemina Facti" (see item 54). Also with Samuel Drake's Boston, 1850 reprint in regular and large paper issues of *News From New-England, Being a True and Last Account of the Present Bloody Wars Carried on Betwixt the Infidels, Natives and the English Christians and Converted Indians of New-England,* originally printed in London in 1676.

28 Peter Williamson
The Life and Adventures of Peter Williamson. Liverpool: T. Troughton, 1807.

"a native of Aberdeen, giving an account of the numerous vicissitudes he had experienced, particularly during his captivity among the Indians, in America, and his sufferings during that time." From a footnote in the narrative: "A tomahawk is a kind of hatchet; made something like our plaisterers' hammer, about two feet long, handle and all. To take up the hatchet (or tomahawk) among them, is to declare war. They generally use it after firing their guns, by rushing on their enemies, and fracturing or cleaving their skulls with it, and very seldom fail of killing at the first blow."

With Edinburgh (1768) edition: *The Travels of Peter Williamson.*

29 James T. De Shields
Cynthia Ann Parker. St. Louis: Printed for the Author, 1886.

"The story of her capture at the massacre of the inmates of Parker's Fort; of her quarter of a century spent among the Comanches, as the wife of the war chief, Peta Nocona; and of her recapture at the Battle of Pease River, by Captain L.S. Ross, of the Texian Rangers." One of the more unusual captivity stories, Cynthia Ann was the mother of the fierce Comanche chieftain, Quanah Parker. Her name was legendary for generations in the Southwest. See William Reese *[Rachael Plummer's Narrative,* Austin: 1977] for a discussion of the connections between the Parker story, the Clarissa Plummer narrative (item 1) and others.

E. S. Carter
The Life and Adventures of E.S. Carter, Including a Trip Across the Plains and Mountains in 1852. St. Joseph, Mo.: 1896.

30

This narrative is one of travel in New Mexico, as well as an account of the author's life in the California gold fields.

David Menzies
Unheard-of-Sufferings of David Menzies, Amongst the Cherokees, and his Surprising Deliverance; in the anthology, *The Mental Novelist, and Amusing Companion, A Collection of Histories, Essays, & Novels.* London: W. Lane, 1783.

31

A virtual burlesque of a captivity narrative, written more for a fantastical evening's entertainment, than for historical accuracy.

32 *Jonas Pettijohn*
Autobiography, Family History and Various Reminiscences of the Life of Jonas Pettijohn Among the Sioux or Dakota Indians, His Escape During the Massacre of August, 1862. Clay Center, Ks.: Dispatch Printing House, 1890.

With an account of causes that led to the uprising. One of the best later accounts of life on the diminishing frontier and of the great Sioux uprising along the northern Midwest, specifically.

33 *Harriet E. Bishop M'Conkey*
Dakota War Whoop; or Indian Massacres and War in Minnesota. Saint Paul: D.D. Merrill, 1863.

Interspersed with very detailed captivity narratives as well as a now classic, general account of events surrounding the story of this war. (Samuel G. Drake's copy, see item 35.)

With Charles S. Bryant and Abel B. Murch, *A History of the Great Massacre by the Sioux Indians, Including the Personal Narratives of Many Who Escaped.* Saint Peter, Minn.: Wainwright & Son, 1872.

34 *Thomas Jefferys*
The Natural and Civil History of the French Dominions in North and South America. London: Thomas Jefferys, 1760.

". . . with the religion, government, genius, character, manners and customs of the Indians and other inhabitants." Much included on treatment of captives by North American tribes.

Adventures and Sufferings

Samuel G. Drake
The History of Philip's War, Commonly called the Great Indian War, of 1675 and 1676. Exeter, N.H.: J.&B. Williams,1836.

35

Containing numerous examples of persons 'carried into captivity.' One of the early founders of the New England Historic Genealogical Society, Drake as a bookseller and historian collected enough material for many studies of the early Indian wars and for the history of Indian captivities to his time. He edited many of the accounts stretching back to Cotton Mather's day. With Drake's edition of William Hubbard's *History of the Indian Wars of New England.* Roxbury, Mass.: Woodward, 1865.

Charles Beatty
The Journal of a Two-Months Tour, With a View of Promoting Religion Among the Frontier Inhabitants of Pennsylvania. Edinburgh: T. Maccliesh, 1798.

36

With descriptions of the frontier wars with Delaware and Shawnee tribes. With Charles Thomson's *An Enquiry Into the Causes of the Alienation of the Delaware and Shawanese Indians From the British Interest, and Into the Measures Taken for Recovering Their Friendship.* London: J. Wilkie, 1759: "We have already experienced the Cruelties of an Indian War, and there are more instances than one to show they are capable of being our most useful Friends or our most dangerous Enemies."

THE INDIAN CAPTIVE.

A NARRATIVE

OF THE

ADVENTURES AND SUFFERINGS

OF

MATTHEW BRAYTON,

IN HIS

THIRTY-FOUR YEARS OF CAPTIVITY

AMONG THE

INDIANS OF NORTH-WESTERN AMERICA.

CLEVELAND, O.:
FAIRBANKS, BENEDICT & CO., PRINTERS, HERALD OFFICE.
1860.

ADVENTURES AND SUFFERINGS

Other Captivity Narratives

and Books Possessing Indian Captivity Narrative Content in the St. Louis Mercantile Library

"Shawnee Village" From William Pidgeon's *Traditions of De-Coo-Dah, and Antiquarian Researches.* (London: Sampson Low, 1853.)

Adventures and Sufferings

John Tanner — 37
A Narrative of the Captivity and Adventures of John Tanner During Thirty Years Residence Among the Indians in the Interior of North America. (New York: G.&C. Carvill, 1830.) Edited by Edwin James. Exhibited with the Paris (1835) edition in two volumes.

Baron Louis-Armand Lahontan — 38
Nouveaux Voyages de Mr le Baron de Lahontan dans l' Amerique Septentrionale. (Hague: Freres l'Honore, 1703.) Copy of E.G. Squier, noted early Americanist and ethnologist, with early St. Louis area pioneer and Baptist clergyman, John Mason Peck's copy in English: *New Voyages to North-America.* (London: J. Osborn, 1735) in two volumes.

Henry Timberlake — 39
The Memoirs of Lieut. Henry Timberlake. (London: Ridley and Henderson, 1765.) With the Paris (1797) edition. First eyewitness account of the Tennessee country.

Francesco Giuseppe Bressani — 40
Relation Abregee de Quelques Missions des Peres de la Compagnie de Jesus dans La Nouvelle-France. (Montreal: Des Presses a Vapeur de John Lovell, 1852.) Later Canadian printing of a 1653 Macerata edition of events which took place in the Iroquois country in 1644. See Kephart's translation, as well as a discussion of Bressani in Jaenen's *Friend and Foe; Aspects of French-Amerindian Cultural Contact in the Sixteenth and Seventeenth Centuries.* From the library of John Mason Peck.

J. H. Alexander — 41
Indian Horrors of the Fifties. Story and Life of the Only Known Captive of the Indian Horrors of Sixty Years Ago. (Synarep, Wash.: Alexander, 1916.)

ADVENTURES AND SUFFERINGS

42 *Richard and Catherine Poe Bard*
Captivity of Richard Bard, Esq., and His Wife, Catharine Poe Bard. (Chambersburg: Conococheague Genealogical Society, 1904.) Occurred in 1758, and came down through the family and by the edition of Pritts.

43 *Matthew Brayton*
The Indian Captive. Narrative of the Adventures and Sufferings of Matthew Brayton in His Thirty-Four Years of Captivity Among the Indians of North-Western America. (Cleveland: Fairbanks, Benedict & Co., 1860.)

44 *John Giles*
Memoirs of Odd Adventures, Strange Deliverances, etc. in the Captivity of John Giles, Commander of the Garrison on Saint George River, in the District of Maine. (Cincinnati: Spiller & Gates, 1869.) A 1736 account reprinted.

45 *Peter Milet*
Captivity of Father Peter Milet, S.J. Among the Oneida Indians. (NewYork: 1888.) 1689-94 account.

46 *Benjamin Gilbert*
A Narrative of the Captivity and Sufferings of Benjamin Gilbert and His Family. (Lancaster, Pa.: 1890.) A 1780 account. Originally edited by William Walton in 1784.

47 *Charles Johnston*
A Narrative of the Incidents Attending the Capture, Detention, and Ransom of Charles Johnston of Botetourt County, Virginia, Who was Made Prisoner by the Indians, on the River Ohio, in the Year 1790. (New-York: J.&J. Harper, 1827.)

Adventures and Sufferings

John F. Meginness — 48
Biography of Frances Slocum, The Lost Sister of Wyoming. A Complete Narrative of Her Captivity and Wanderings Among the Indians. (Williamsport, Pa.: Heller, 1891.)

Minnie Buce Carrigan — 49
Captured by the Indians; Reminiscences of Pioneer Life in Minnesota. (Buffalo Lake, Minn.: 1912.)

Darius B. Cook — 50
Six Months Among Indians, Wolves and Other Wild Animals, In the Forests of Allegan County, Mich., In the Winter of 1839 and 1840. The Exploits of Tecumseh and Other Chiefs, Their Cruelty to Captives. (Niles, Mich.: Niles Mirror, 1889.)

James E. Seaver — 51
Deh-he-wa-mis: or a Narrative of the Life of Mary Jemison, Otherwise Called the White Woman, Who was Taken Captive by the Indians in 1755; and Who Continued with Them Seventy-Eight Years, Carefully Taken from Her Own Words. (London: Tegg, 1847.)

John Reynolds — 52
The Pioneer History of Illinois, Containing the Discovery in 1673, and the History of the Country to the Year 1818, When the State Government was Organized. (Belleville, Ill.: Randall, 1852.) Reynolds' most lasting work, often collected from notes and interviews with early settlers, is the best example of early local history, replete with among other accounts, that of captivity versions. With three others, Chipman Turner's *The Pioneer Period of Western New York* (Buffalo: 1888), Hervey Scott's *Complete History of Fairfield County, Ohio* (Columbus: 1877), and U.J. Jones' *History of the Early Settlement of the Juniata Valley* (Harrisburg, Pa.: 1889.)

ADVENTURES AND SUFFERINGS

53 *Alvar Nuñez Cabeza de Vaca*
The Narrative of Alvar Nuñez Cabeca de Vaca. (Washington: 1851.) The Smith translation. Presented by G. W. Riggs to E. George Squier. Early English translation of the 1555 Spanish original.

54 *Hannah Duston*
Captivity Narrative of Hannah Duston, Related by Cotton Mather, John Greenleaf Whittier, Nathaniel Hawthorne and Henry David Thoreau, Four Versions of Events in 1697, Interspersed With Thirty-five Wood-Block Prints by Richard Bosman. (San Francisco: Arion Press, 1987.) With Robert Caverly's *Heroism of Hannah Duston, Together With The Indian Wars of New England.* (Boston: Russell & Co., 1874.) The story, passed down and retold many times, of the early heroine, who turned the tables on her captors, dispatching them as they slept and escaping into legend and myth.

Item 54

55 *Mary Rowlandson*
Narrative of the Captivity and Removes of Mrs. Mary Rowlandson, Who was Taken by the Indians at the Destruction of Lancaster, in 1676. (Lancaster: Carter, Andrews, 1828.)

56 *John Jewitt*
A Narrative of the Adventures and Sufferings of John R. Jewitt; Only Survivor of the Crew of the Ship Boston, During a Captivity of Nearly

Adventures and Sufferings

Three Years Among the Savages of Nootka Sound. (Middletown: Loomis & Richards, 1815.) Part of the St. Louis Lyceum Library, the holdings of which came to the Mercantile Library in 1851.

John Leith — 57
A Short Biography of John Leith, With a Brief Account of His Life Among the Indians. (Cincinnati: Robert Clarke, 1883.) Butterfield edition.

Robert Eastburn — 58
The Dangers and Sufferings of Robert Eastburn, and His Deliverance from Indian Captivity. (Cleveland: Burrows, 1904.) Spears edition of 1758 original.

Nehemiah How — 59
A Narrative of the Captivity of Nehemiah How in 1745-1747. (Cleveland: Burrows, 1904.) Paltsits edition of 1748 original.

John Williams — 60
The Redeemed Captive Returning to Zion or the Captivity and Deliverance of Rev. John Williams of Deerfield. (Springfield, Mass.: Huntting Co., 1908.) Reprint of Sixth edition, 1795. With *What Befell Stephen Williams in His Captivity*. Sheldon's 1889 edition.

Fanny Kelly — 61
Narrative of My Captivity Among the Sioux Indians. (Hartford: Mutual Publishing Co., 1871.)

Alexander Berghold — 62
The Indians' Revenge; or, Days of Horror. Some Appalling Events in the History of the Sioux. (San Francisco: P.J. Thomas, 1891.)

ADVENTURES AND SUFFERINGS

63 *Herman Lehmann*
Nine Years Among the Indians, 1870-1879; The Story of the Captivity and Life of a Texan Among the Indians. (Austin: Von Boeckmann-Jones Co., 1927.)

64 *James B. Finley*
Life Among the Indians or, Personal Reminiscences and Historical Incidents Illustrative of Indian Life and Character. (Cincinnati: Cranston & Curts, 1868.)

65 *Edwin Eastman*
Seven and Nine Years Among the Camanches and Apaches. (Jersey City, N.J.: Johnson, 1873.)

66 *Stephen R. Riggs*
Mary and I, Forty Years with the Sioux. (Boston: Congregational House, 1887.)

67 *William Biggs*
Narrative of the Captivity of William Biggs Among the Kickapoo Indians in Illinois in 1788. (Originally published in 1826; reprinted in 1902 by The Illinois State Historical Library; reprinted in 1922 by Charles Heartman as part of Heartman's Historical Series of which this is a complimentary copy from Heartman to the Mercantile.)

68 *T. M. Newson*
Thrilling Scenes Among the Indians. With a Graphic Description of Custer's Last Fight with Sitting Bull. (Chicago: Belford, Clarke & Co., 1884.)

Adventures and Sufferings

Peter Ogden — **69**
Traits of American-Indian Life and Character, by a Fur Trader. (London: Smith, Elder, 1853.)

William Pote, Jr. — **70**
The Journal of Captain William Pote. Jr. During His Captivity in the French and Indian War, From May, 1745, to August, 1747. (New York: Dodd, Mead, 1896.)

Zadock Steele — **71**
The Indian Captive: or a Narrative of the Captivity and Sufferings of Zadock Steele, Related by Himself, To Which is Prefixed an Account of the Burning of Royalton. (Springfield, Mass.: Huntting, 1908.)

Peter Ronan — **72**
Historical Sketch of the Flathead Indian Nation From the Year 1813 to 1890. (Helena: Journal Publishing Co., 1890.)

A. W. Patterson — **73**
History of the Backwoods; or, The Region of the Ohio: Authentic, From the Earliest Accounts. (Pittsburgh: 1843.)

Cadwallader Colden — **74**
The History of the Five Indian Nations of Canada. (London: T. Osborne, 1747.)

James Smith — **75**
An Account of the Remarkable Occurrences in the Life and Travels of Colonel James Smith. (Philadelphia: Grigg & Elliot, 1834.) With the Cincinnati reprint of 1870 and Dodge's *Red Men of the Ohio Valley* (Springfield, Oh.: 1860.)

ADVENTURES AND SUFFERINGS

76 *Benjamin Drake*
The Life and Adventures of Black Hawk; with Sketches of Keokuk, The Sac and Fox Indians and the Late Black Hawk War. (Cincinnati: Conclin, 1849.) With the 1856 edition and with an early epic poem on the subject of the great Indian leader, Smith's *Ma-Ka-Tai-Me-She-Kia-Kiak or Black Hawk and Scenes in the West.* (New York: Kearny, 1848.)

77 *Benjamin Drake*
Life of Tecumseh, and of His Brother The Prophet; with a Historical Sketch of the Shawanoe Indians. (Cincinnati: Morgan, 1841.)

78 *Joseph Pritts*
Mirror of Olden Time Border Life . . . to Which are Added Personal Narratives of Captivities and Escapes – of Strange and Thrilling Adventures – Personal Prowess, etc. (Abingdon, Va.: Miles, 1849.) With the Chambersburg, Pa. German edition of 1839.

79 *Alphonso Wetmore*
Gazetteer of the State of Missouri. (St. Louis: Keemle [New York: Harper], 1837.) Containing the famous account of "A Pawnee Sacrifice."

80 *James Macaulay*
Grey Hawk: Life and Adventures Among the Red Indians. (Philadelphia: Lippincott & Co., 1883.)

81 *John Gilmary Shea*
Perils of the Ocean and Wilderness: or Narratives of Shipwreck and Indian Captivity. (Boston: Donahoe, 1857.)

82 *John McLean*
The Indians of Canada: Their Manners and Customs. (London: Kelly, 1892.)

ADVENTURES AND SUFFERINGS

Herbert Milton Sylvester — 83
Indian Wars of New England. 3 Volumes. (Boston: W.B. Clarke, 1910.)

Thomas L. McKenney and James Hall — 84
The Indian Tribes of North America, with Biographical Sketches and Anecdotes of the Principal Chiefs. (Edinburgh: Grant, 1933.) 3 Volumes. The Hodge edition.

P. F. X. de Charlevoix — 85
Histoire et Description Generale de la Nouvelle France. 2 Volumes. (Paris: Nyon, 1744.)

Pierre Pouchot — 86
Memoir Upon the Late War in North America Between the French and English, 1755-60. (Roxbury, Mass.: 1866.) Hough edition, 2 Volumes.

John Knox — 87
An Historical Journal of the Campaigns in North-America for the Years 1757, 1758, 1759, and 1760. 2 Volumes. (London: 1769.)

Henry Rowe Schoolcraft — 88
Historical and Statistical Information Respecting the History, Condition and Prospects of the Indian Tribes of the United States. 6 Volumes. (Philadelphia: Lippincott, Grambo & Co., 1851-1857.) With Illustrations by Seth Eastman.

John Long — 89
Voyages and Travels of an Indian Interpreter and Trader, Describing the Manners and Customs of the North American Indians. (London: 1791.)

ADVENTURES AND SUFFERINGS

90 *Alexander V. Blake*
Anecdotes of the American Indians. (New York: Blake, 1844.)

91 *George Mogridge*
The History, Manners and Customs of the North American Indians. (Philadelphia: American Sunday-School Union, [1845-1850].)

92 *Augustus Ward Loomis*
Scenes in the Indian Country. (Philadelphia: Presbyterian Board of Publication, 1859.)

93 *Samuel G. Goodrich*
The Manners, Customs, and Antiquities of the Indians of North and South America. (Boston: Taggard and Thompson, 1864.)

94 *George Turner*
Traits of Indian Character; as Generally Applicable to the Aborigines of North America. (Philadelphia: Key & Biddle, 1836.)

95 *Minnie Myrtle (Anna C. Miller)*
The Iroquois; or The Bright Side of Indian Character. (New York: Appleton, 1855.)

96 *George P. Belden*
Belden, The White Chief; or Twelve Years Among the Wild Indians of the Plains. (Cincinnati: Starr & Co., 1875.) With James Brisbin's *Stories of the Plains*. (St. Louis: Anchor, 1881.)

97 *John W. DeForest*
History of the Indians of Connecticut from the Earliest Known Period to 1850. (Hartford: Hamersley, 1851.)

ADVENTURES AND SUFFERINGS

De Benneville Randolph Keim — 98
Sheridan's Troopers on the Borders: A Winter Campaign on the Plains. (Philadelphia: Claxton, 1870.)

Charles de Wolf Brownell — 99
The Indian Races of North and South America. (New York: American Subscription House, 1856.)

A. R. Fulton — 100
The Red Men of Iowa; Being a History of the Various Aboriginal Tribes Whose Homes were in Iowa; Sketches of Chiefs, Traditions, Indian Hostilities, Incidents and Reminiscences. (Des Moines: Mills, 1882.)

J. Lee Humfreville — 101
Twenty Years Among Our Hostile Indians. (New York: Hunter, 1899.)

Daniel W. Jones — 102
Forty Years Among the Indians; A True Yet Thrilling Narrative of the Author's Experiences Among the Natives. (Salt Lake City: Juvenile Instructor Office, 1890.)

Mary H. Eastman — 103
The American Aboriginal Portfolio. (Philadelphia: Lippincott, Grambo & Co., 1853.)

Mary H. Eastman — 104
Chicora and Other Regions of the Conquerors and the Conquered. (Philadelphia: Lippincott, Grambo, and Co., 1854.)

105 *Frank Triplett*
Conquering the Wilderness; or New Pictorial History of the Life and Times of the Pioneer Heroes and Heroines of America. (New York and St. Louis: Thompson, 1883.)

106 *William Livingston*
A Review of the Military Operations in North America; From the Commencement of the French Hostilities on the Frontiers of Virginia in 1753, to the Surrender of Oswego, on the 14th of August, 1756. (London: Dodsley, 1757.)

107 *Henry Rowe Schoolcraft*
Western Scenes and Reminiscences: Together with Thrilling Legends and Traditions of the Red Men of the Forest. (Buffalo: Derby, 1853.)

108 *John McIntosh*
The Origin of the North American Indians. (New York: Sheldon, 1855.)

109 *Samuel G. Drake*
Biography and History of the Indians of North America. (Boston: Antiquarian Institute, 1837.)

110 *John Heckewelder*
A Narrative of the Mission of the United Brethren Among the Delaware and Mohegan Indians. (Philadelphia: M'Carty & Davis, 1820.) With the 1907 edition and with the Göttingen edition of *An Account of the Indian Nations, Who Once Inhabited Pennsylvania, etc.* (1818,1821).

111 *C. R. Tuttle*
History of the Border Wars of Two Centuries, Embracing A Narrative of the Wars with the Indians from 1750 to 1876. (Madison, Wis.: Pennock, 1876.)

ADVENTURES AND SUFFERINGS

112 *George Henry Loskiel*
History of the Mission of the United Brethren Among the Indians in North America. (London: Brethren's Society for the Furtherance of the Gospel, 1794.) With the Swedish edition (1792) and the German edition (1789).

113 *James O. Lewis*
The Aboriginal Portfolio. (Philadelphia: 1835-36.)

114 *Edwardsville Spectator*
Volume VII, no. 50, new series. (Edwardsville, Ill.: September 29, 1826.) From John Mason Peck's library. Column 3: "Alexander O'Connell's Escape from Five Indians." 'This story we have from a respectable gentleman, now living in this neighborhood, who was an intimate friend of Mr. M'Connell *[sic]*." (Events which supposedly occurred in 1781.)

POCAHONTAS INTERCEDING WITH POWHATTAN IN BEHALF OF COL. SMITH.

Item 78

115 *John Smith*
De Gedenkwaardige Reizen Vanden Beroemden Capiteyn Johan Smith na Virginien. (Leyden: 1707.) Separate from Pieter vander Aa's *NaaukeurigeVersameling der gedenkwaardigste Zee en Land-Reysen.* (Volume 23). Bought single volume from W.H. Miner in 1917. ("the memorable travels of the renowned Captain John Smith to Virginia")

Adventures and Sufferings

116 *J.B. Jones*
The Warpath: A Narrative of Adventures in the Wilderness, (Philadelphia: Lippincott and Co., 1874)

117 *Augustus Lynch Mason*
Indian Wars and Famous Frontiersmen. (Merriam: 1904)

118 *Henry Davenport Northrup*
Indian Horrors, or Massacres of the Red Men; A Thrilling Narrative of Bloody Wars with Merciless and Revengeful Savages. (s.n.; n.d.)

119 *Frank H. Norton*
The Days of Daniel Boone; A Romance of the Dark and Bloody Ground. (New York: American News, 1883)

120 *Dr. Benjamin Dolbeare*
A Narrative of the Captivity and Suffering of Dolly Webster Among the Comanche Indians in Texas with an Account of the Massacre of John Webster and his Party, as Related by Mrs. Webster. (New Haven: Yale, 1986)

121 *Emerson Bennett*
Ella Barnwell; A Historical Romance of Border Life. (Cincinnati: James, 1853)

122 *Robert Montgomery Bird*
Nick of the Woods, or the Jibbenainosay; a Tale of Kentucky. (New York: Redfield, 1858)

ADVENTURES AND SUFFERINGS

{Jervis Cutler}
A Topographical Description of the State of Ohio, Indiana Territory, and Louisiana...To Which is Added, an Interesting Journal of Mr. Chas. Le Raye, while a Captive with the Sioux Nation, on the Waters of the Missouri River. (Boston: Charles Williams, 1812)
123

James F. M'Gaw
Philip Seymour, or Pioneer Life in Richland County, Ohio, Founded in Facts. (Mansfield: Brinkerhoff, 1858)
124

Isaac V.D. Heard
History of the Sioux War. (New York: Harper, 1864)
125

Bennett, Emerson
Forest and Prairie; or Life on the Frontier. (Philadelphia: Potter, 1860)
126

J.B. Jones
Wild Western Scenes: A Narrative of Adventures in the Western Wilderness. (Philadelphia: Lippincott, 1871)
127

John S. Robb
Kaam; or Daylight; The Arapahoe Half-Breed. A Tale of the Rocky Mountains. (Boston: Jones, 1848).
128

Indian Anecdotes and Barbarities
Being a Description of Their Customs and Deeds of Cruelty. With an Account of the Captivity, Sufferings and Heroic Conduct of Many Who Have Fallen into Their Hands, or Who Have Defended Themselves from Savage Vengeance; all Illustrating the Traits of Indian Character. (Barre, Mass.: Gazette Office, 1837)
129

130 *Isaac Zane*
Report of the Committee To Whom Was Referred on the 7th Instant; the Petition of Isaac Zane. (1802)

131 *George Henry Sylvester*
Just Returned from Indian Captivity. (undated photograph, ca. 1870).

132 *Elihu Hoyt*
A Brief Sketch of the First Settlement of Deerfield, Mass. (Greenfield: Fogg, 1833) [with the accounts of Jonathan Hoyt and John Williams].

133 *Mary Smith*
An Affecting Narrative of the Captivity and Sufferings of Mary Smith. (Williamsburgh, Mass.: Whitman, 1818)

134 *Josiah Priest*
Stories of Early Settlers in the Wilderness: Embracing the Life of Mrs. Priest. (Albany:Munsell, 1837)

135 *Hannah Swanton*
The Casco Captive, or the Catholic Religion in Canada, and its Influence on the Indians in Maine. (Boston: Massachusetts Sabbath School Society, 1839)

136 *Joseph Eastburn*
Memoirs. (Philadelphia: Mentx, 1828) With an account of the captivity of his father, Robert Eastburn; see Item 58)

Benjamin Gilbert — 137
A Narrative of the Captivity and Sufferings of Benjamin Gilbert and His Family Who Were Surprised by the Indians, and Taken from Their Farms, on the Frontiers of Pennsylvania in the Spring of 1780. (London: James Phillips, 1790) See Item 46.

Susannah Rowson — 138
Charlotte Temple; a Tale of Truth. (New York: Leavitt and Allen, 1853)

James H. McMechen — 139
Legends of the Ohio Valley or Thrilling Incidents of Indian Warfare. Truth Stranger Than Fiction. (Wheeling: West Virginia Printers, 1888)

John C. Shafford — 140
Narrative of the Extraordinary Life of John C. Shafford – the Dutch Hermit. (New York: Carpenter, 1840) and a second printing, same place and publisher, 1842.

Jeremy Belknap — 141
The History of New Hampshire. (Boston: Bradford and Bear, 1813) 3 vols. (with the Rev. Bunker Gay's version of the Jemima Howe narrative).

Grace E. Meredith — 142
Girl Captives of the Cheyenne; A True Story of the Capture and Rescue of Four Pioneer Girls. (Los Angeles: Gem Publishing, 1927)

ADVENTURES AND SUFFERINGS

143 *John Niles Hubbard*
Sketches of the Life and Adventures of Moses Van Campen, a Surviving Officer of the Army of the Revolution. (Dansville, N. Y.: Stevens, 1841. (Containing the 1780 captivity of Major Van Campen on the New York frontier).

144 *Henry Howe*
Historical Collections of the Great West. (Cincinnati: Morgan, 1853)

145 *Edward S. Ellis*
The Indian Wars of the United States, from the First Settlement at Jamestown, in 1607, to the Close of the Great Uprising of 1890-91. (Chicago: Kenyon, 1892)

146 *Cecil Hartley*
Life and Adventures of Lewis Wetzel, the Virginia Ranger. (Philadelphia: Evans, 1860) Illustrated by G.G. White.

147 *Henry White*
Indian Battles; with Incidents in the Early History of New England. (New York: Evans, 1859)

148 *Joseph Bartlett*
A Narrative of the Captivity of Joseph Bartlett Among the French and Indians, written by himself. (Printed for the purchaser, 1807)

149 *Hugh D. Corwin*
Comanche and Kiowa Captives in Oklahoma and Texas. (Guthrie: Cooperative Publishing Co., 1959)

Adventures and Sufferings

Appendix 1

*Early Graphic Artists and the Indian Captivity Narrative –
A Contribution to the History of American Book Illustration*

Before many books in America possessed illustrations of any sort, printers added exciting, melodramatic and lurid detail to the many Indian captivity narratives which they published through numerous illustrations gathered from contemporary artists. Indeed, some of the first illustrated books in America were captivity narratives. As if the graphic imagery detailed in the prose were not enough to set the tone of these works, it was almost as if pictures could add to the veracity of the extraordinary and frightening tales.

See Item 13. Often, a captivity was accompanied with a woodcut engraving depicting a harrowing, grief filled procession on the frontier.

ADVENTURES AND SUFFERINGS

In the matter of origins, works of travel and description in America were some of the earliest illustrated books in the New World, and these texts often would depict the fascinating, original inhabitants of North America – their customs, their ornaments and arms, their homes and way of life – all of these aspects of Indian lore were of perennial interest to Europeans. Artists and writers such as White, Lahontan or Lafiteau fostered a centuries' long diet of illustration for readers in the colonies and the Old World.

The illustration of captivity narratives grew out of this tradition, in part. The grisly illustrations accompanying saints' lives and martyrdoms and the violence of the religious wars between Catholic and Protestant during the Reformation and the early modern historical age may also be considered an important precedent in the captivity iconography.

By the late eighteenth century and certainly throughout the nineteenth, early engravers and anonymous woodcut artists were creating a sub-genre of illustration for the captivity narrative – one which had its own conventions and symbols, and one which at times could be interchangeable from narrative to narrative. Virtually no illustration was created by an eyewitness in this period – many were crude, violent depictions – "penny dreadful" pieces or caricatures, such as one would see in early American broadside or almanac illustration.

Mrs. Howe's babe wrested from her by the Indians.

The Indians shooting at Miss Lovell.

See Item 129, crude woodcuts underscored the stark, uninhibited violence of the early nineteenth century captivity tales. Works such as these scenes anticipate the pulp genre horror stories of the early twentieth century.

ADVENTURES AND SUFFERINGS

See Item 129 (anonymous artist)

This type of art gradually came to coexist with more polished, academy trained artists' depictions – Felix Darley's work is perhaps the most famous in this regard. Darley was a great student of the old Indian captivity narratives in America, and he used the Indian as a way to create a frontier myth, a legend and a heroic depiction of the perils of the frontier pioneers, all, seemingly, without ever traveling West. He did this to curry favor with American publishers looking to illustrate the works of the first American novelists – often writers who used native Americans for subject matter. It is no accident that writers such as Irving and Cooper preferred their editions to be illustrated by Darley – and his work was eventually sought by non-fiction writers such as Parkman, or even by the newspapers, such as *Harper's Weekly*.

Adventures and Sufferings

A famous engraving by Felix Darley, strongly related to a design by painter, Carl Wimar.

ADVENTURES AND SUFFERINGS

Stereotypical engravings by Felix Darley in the mid-nineteenth century often depicted the captivity genre.

Adventures and Sufferings

Felix Darley – from a wood engraving in *Harper's Weekly*, mid-nineteenth century.

Darley's work was so popular that painters such as Bingham, Wimar, and John Mix Stanley were inspired to create famous canvasses depicting captivities. Darley collaborated with other artists such as Karl Bodmer to create highly artistic, marketable prints of captivity accounts.

Adventures and Sufferings

The Perils of Our Forefathers **from a painting by F.A. Chapman, engraved by John C. McRae, 1859.**

Adventures and Sufferings

Capture of the Daughters of Daniel Boone and Callaway by the Indians from a design after Karl Bodmer, by Darley, 1857.

ADVENTURES AND SUFFERINGS

Aus Daniel Boone's Leben.

See Item 20. A German version of the Capture of Daniel Boone's Daughters.

Adventures and Sufferings

"After the Surprise"

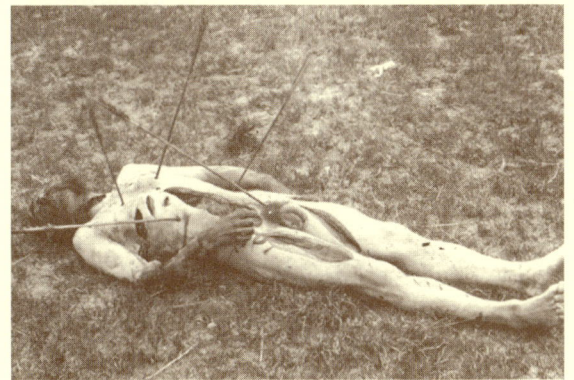

Alexander Gardner. *On the Great Plains in Kansas, Sergeant of the Escort,* from *Across the Continent on the Kansas Pacific Railroad,* 1868. (Barriger Collection, Mercantile Library)

"Running the Gauntlet," Item 117

ADVENTURES AND SUFFERINGS

Coupled with the work of the engravers, increasingly, came the work of photographers such as Alexander Gardner and Edward Curtis. Gardner's work on "Death on the Plains" in *Across the Continent on the Kansas and Pacific Railroad (1868)* does profoundly what most true captivity narratives in prose did not – show the outcome of one who did not make it back, simply, to relate his or her narrative. Instead, this captive becomes in death what artists of all kinds increasingly saw as the visual impact of a sacrifice to the taming of the frontier. Photo journalism had arrived to the genre.

In the twentieth century, the captivity narrative was almost solely kept alive by private presses and the art of the fine illustrated edition – the work of Eric Gill in illustrating the life and captivity of the Jesuit martyr, Father Brebeuf (1938), or the multiple edition of the accounts of the Hannah Duston narrative created by the Arion Press (1987) are noteworthy examples of the ways in which the captivity narrative has continued to find an audience in a multi-media sense.

See Item 54. Frontispiece of Item 54 (left), *Dashed Out Brains* **(right)**

Adventures and Sufferings

A Bookplate design by Eric Gill, early 20th century.

ADVENTURES AND SUFFERINGS

THE TRAVELS OF FATHER JEAN AMONG THE HURONS CRIBED BY HIMSELF ED FROM THE FRENCH

THE GOLDEN COCKEREL

Book design by Eric Gill, 1938.

& SUFFERINGS
DE BRÉBEUF ✝
OF CANADA AS DES-
EDITED & TRANSLAT-
AND LATIN BY THEO-
DORE BESTERMAN

PRESS MCMXXXVIII

ADVENTURES AND SUFFERINGS

The graphic or visual representations of the past are important in that they resonate in the paintings of twentieth century Western artists, such as Russell, Schreyvogel, Farney, Couse, Remington and others. These paintings and the analogue narratives, on which they are in part based, in turn have influenced scores of motion pictures – from John Ford to Michael Mann – and hundreds of television "westerns" over the past half century. Whether handled as high art in literature, painting or film, or as popular culture – from the old dime novels to melodramatic screenplay, all of these forms – including the graphic, printed engravings and woodcuts, bear evocative witness to the power and resilience of the captivity narrative as an archetypical compendium of literary and visual images through the past five centuries.

Design from the 1991 edition of Rupert Noral Richardson's *The Comanche Barrier to South Plains Settlement*.

ADVENTURES AND SUFFERINGS

A typical dime novel of the early twentieth century.

Appendix 2

Facsimile of a Regional Narrative: The James Taylor Narrative

"A Narrative of the Horrid Massacre By the Indians of the Wife and Children of the Christian Hermit, A Resident of Missouri With a Full Account of His Life and Sufferings, Never Before Published" (St. Louis: Whiting, 1840) See Item 6.

The following captivity has many of the typical passages which such works exhibited for hundreds of years – all the way back to Puritan or colonial Virginia times. Taking place in early Missouri during the War of 1812, it possesses a sense of gloom and tension which equaled many of the most violent narratives of the period.

Omens and foreshadowing. Mockery by a seemingly invincible and satanic foe. The little cabin in the wilderness clearing, overgrown from the inactivity brought on by impending danger. The attack and the savage murder of the pioneer family. And the Christian resignation to accept the Lord's will, to become a grieving supplicant to God in the wilderness – the escaped captive's desire to live alone as a frontier hermit in deep sadness and overpowering memory of one's loss, a destroyed and sacrificial lamb to the taming of the nation – all of this is possessed in the James Taylor narrative – one which reaches to the earliest captivities in its narrative conventions, and yet one which has the spell binding immediacy of a thrilling, original adventure story.

Surely a work like this and the following "Deposition" below represent what R.W.G. Vail referred to as "the voice of the old frontier" in his famous collection of Rosenbach lectures. [see bibliography]. We listen to these old, shocking stories with rapt attention – with fear, with disbelief to the violence visited upon man by man. And yet, is not there something echoing down to us in such voices in the

American past? Are not the thousands of captivity narratives a defining issue for us as Americans? A country forged in the violent wars between New World cultures may forever continue to define its relation to the world of nations and cultures in protectively violent terms, necessitating costs and sacrifice for long established beliefs in our "American-ness", in democracy, in liberty.

The plaintive voice of the frontier in these great, powerful narratives may indeed be a siren song – may we not be trapped to this day in sometimes defining the nation in the violent terms of a folk memory learned when the nation was young? The risk has always been present. That seems to be why the captivity narrative is so powerfully commemorative. So genealogical. So evocative. Americans studying their own past. The reading of Indian captivity narratives may just be a cautionary to the future, not merely an exercise in antiquarianism. This is why they seem to have never been forgotten in our culture – they resonate with a relevancy to every American generation which earnestly attempts to define what it means to be American.

The frontispiece to the Taylor narrative, the village of "Adron" Missouri.

A

NARRATIVE

OF THE

HORRID MASSACRE   F804
                  T21
BY THE INDIANS,

OF THE WIFE AND CHILDREN

OF THE

CHRISTIAN HERMIT,

A RESIDENT OF MISSOURI,

WITH

A FULL ACCOUNT OF HIS LIFE AND SUFFERINGS,

NEVER BEFORE PUBLISHED.

St. LOUIS:
LEANDER W. WHITING & Co.
1840.

NARRATIVE.

In the Northern part of Missouri, several miles from any village, or inhabitant, lives one of the most odd, and apparently, most contented and cheerful characters, perhaps, that the world ever afforded. The true name of this person, is James B. Taylor, though commonly known by that of the "*Christian Hermit,*" a name which cannot be ill applied to one who has drunk often of the bitter cup of sorrow, and bore his trials with much of that christian fortitude, which characterised the old Prophets, and Apostles of our Saviour. It is but a short time since that I was induced to call upon him, by a christian friend, (October 10th, 1839.) After riding about 3 hours, among the mountains, westerly from the village of Aldren,* we came to his rough dwelling, situated upon the side of a mountain, in which he has spent ten years. His humble habitation, composed of logs laid together, is one of his own construction, and where he informed me he has dwelt alone since he lost his wife and children, who fell victims to the ferocity of a band of savages. As we entered he asked us to be seated, while he would relate to us the scenes through which he had in the Providence of God been called to pass. He narrated his story as follows:

I was born in New York, in the year 1780, where I was married, and lived happily with my family, until the month of July 1810, when forming an acquaintance with David Hinds, a man celebrated for his exploits among the western

---
*See Frontispiece, for a correct view of the village of Adren, with the range of Mountains, on the westerly side of which, is situated the hut of the Christian Hermit.

people, & for being an early settler in that part of the western country which now comprises a portion of the state of Missouri, and also for the bravery displayed by him in the frequent skirmishes which occurred with the Indians in that quarter. We were prevailed on by Hinds to accompany him with his family to that beautiful and justly extolled country ; and although a removal with my family was attended with many inconveniences, yet we finally reached our journey's end in safety. By the advice of Hinds, we took up our abode in a small town where I built a temporary hut to shelter us from the storms, with the intent of building a better one when opportunity offered. The delightful prospect that I should enjoy, undisturbed, my favorite amusement, the chase, as the forest abounded with wild game of almost every kind—was soon blighted. Although the hostile Indians, had met with many serious defeats, yet they were unwilling to bury the hatchet, and continued their depredations, killing and scalping the defenceless inhabitants whenever oportunity offered. The situation of myself and family was extremely dangerous, at this time—for it was not only unsafe to venture far from my cabin in pursuit of game, but it was at the risk of my life that I attempted even to cultivate a few acres of ground. In the spring of 1811 they killed and scalped a man with his daughter and son, only one mile distant from my dwelling, and made captives of one promising young damsel, and one lad of thirteen. A company of whites, of whom I was one, went immediately in pursuit, and overtook them, but as they proved to be double in number to us, we were obliged to return as fast as possible without effecting the liberation of the captives, who as they never returned to their friends, were probably put to death by the savages, in their barbarous manner.

Emboldened by their success in putting their pursuers to flight, they now appeared in still greater numbers, almost daily in view of our little settlement; and the more to torment us they amused themselves by brandishing their tomahawks, and imitating the past groans of our dying friends whom they had taken prisoners, and on whom they had inflicted cruelties too horrible to relate.

It was at this awful moment thought advisable to form a union of all the men under our control that could be collected, in order to save ourselves and families from sharing the fate of our brethren. Two hundred men were speedily collected, who, under the command of David Hinds, Carns and myself, marched in pursuit. We had penetrated into the wilderness about 20 miles before we overtook them. We fell in with a large body of them whom we put to flight after a short skirmish ; and being ignorant of their numbers, we crossed a branch of the Missouri river in pursuit of them. The engagement was a warm one and lasted an hour, when being overpowered by our little band, they were again put to flight, losing thirty of their men. After this engagement, we became very much fatigued, but being unwilling to give up the contest until we had secured them all, we imprudently pursued after them again and were overpowered, losing eighty-five of our men, some having been taken prisoners and others killed. Among the slain were Hinds and Carns, and a son of the former. We were informed about four days afterwards by one of our company, (who had been taken prisoner but had contrived to make his escape,) that the savages on finding out that their loss was eight more than ours, gave up eight of our men to be put to death, after their savage manner by tying them to a post and sticking them full of splinters made of pine knots and setting fire to them, by which they were gradually consumed. This fatal and unexpected defeat had a great effect in damp'ning the spirits of the survivors. Among the dead were some of the first men of our little settlement. Many widows were thereby made, and for many days did the air ring with the groans of the afflicted, while mourning and sorrow sat upon the countenances of almost every person. Six days afterwards having heard that the Indians had returned to their own settlements, satisfied with the booty they had taken from us, we returned to the battle ground, and such a sight I never wish to lay my eyes upon again. There were the dead scalped and stripped of their clothing, and the bodies of some torn to pieces and half eaten up by the wild beasts. We interred in two graves the mangled bodies of our friends, to await the resurrection morn. We then returned to our homes with sorrowful hearts and sad countenances.

The news of our defeat soon reached the troops stationed on the frontiers, whereupon they sent us reinforcements; with a request that we should pursue these fiends in human shape, to their very settlements; in which expedition I volunteered my services and which was probably the cause of their attack upon my family about six months from that period.

We fell in with a large body of the enemy within a few miles of their village, to which they fled for safety; but finding themselves pursued closely, they fled in every direction, greatly disordered. Agreeably to the command of our officers we set their village on fire and reduced to ashes their deserted houses,—destroyed all of their farms and produce, and took several prisoners; with the loss of only two men on our part. The Indians, on account of the loss of their all, became still more enraged against the Inhabitants, and sought every opportunity to destroy them. A few days afterwards two of them boldly entered the settlement, seized a woman, and was carrying her off, when her cries being heard, which brought several to her assistance, and they were all killed.

After the treaty of peace between England and America had been effected, the Indians finding it was the intention of the troops to employ themselves in making an utter extermination of them, consented to lay down the tomahawk in peace and no longer disturb the peace of the white inhabitants provided they could remain unmolested in their own villages and on their own hunting grounds, which we agreed they might do. And so strong did the savages seem to consider the treaty, that I was led to trust myself and family out into the wilderness farther than was prudent, throwing myself off my guard and removing a great distance from any fortified settlement. The ground in the settlement where I went was very rich although uncultivated and abounding with game of all kinds. I, like the rest of my brethren who lived there, were obliged to trust to the honor of the Indians as were more than two miles distant from any white settlement. They for several months appeared as friendly as if there never had been any difficulty between us, and it seemed to me that nothing would again occur to mar our happiness. But alas! the ways of God are different from man'sways. When out upon an excursion one day, I unfortunately met with an Indian, who recognized me as one of the party who had destroyed their village, and even hinted that I struck him on that occasion with a tomahawk I had with me. This belief of his operated to my disadvantage. It even caused the destruction of my family.

About ten days subsequent to my interview with this Indian, one morning a little after daylight, my family was dreadfully alarmed upon discovering a savage secreted in a thicket a little way from the house, who was painted in a style most horrible to behold, and armed with a tomahawk, scalping knife, and bow and arrow. He now uttered a loud yell, which directly aroused 9 or 10 more, who joined him, and they all at the moment rushed from the forest, and with a shout and uplifted tomahawk's approached my dwelling— At that instant I had arose from my bed, and was dressing myself. My poor alarmed family had but just time to reach the house and fasten the doors, before the savages were pounding and demanding entrance; but not succeeding there,

2

ADVENTURES AND SUFFERINGS

they soon made a passage through the side of the house, large enough to admit one at a time. Yet they hesitated to enter, for fear of meeting with too warm a reception from us within; and so they adopted a different mode in order to reach us.—There was at the back side of the house a large quantity of straw. This they set fire to, which soon communicated to the building; and it burnt so rapidly, that we were forced to leave the house, or else be consumed by the devouring element—we preferred the former.

My family at that time consisted of my wife, and eight children; four sons, and four daughters. I was the first to leave the house, in order that I might prepare the way for my family; but this I could not accomplish, for no sooner had I made my appearance, than one of the Indians, who knew me, struck me a blow which stunned me for some time; and they supposing me dead, rushed into the house to find my wife and children. At this moment I recovered my senses, and made my way to the forest, where I secreted myself, though in such a manner that I could see what was transpiring. It was a most heart-rending spectacle to me, a parent and husband, in a situation that would not allow me to assist them in the least. My oldest son attempted to escape, but was caught, and his brains dashed out! My second son also made the attempt, but was likewise caught, and while one savage was scalping him, another dashed out his brains!—And oh! my beloved wife, while in the act of escaping, shared a similar fate! And my little daughters, who left the house with their mother were seized by the inhuman monsters, and while they were apparently in the act of tomahawking them, they fell on their knees and implored for mercy, believing that they were about to share a similar fate with the rest. I now felt that this last sacrifice should be at the expense of at least one of their lives, and accordingly took aim with my rifle to shoot; but it missed fire, and it happened well for me that it did, for had it went off, it would have been at the expense of my life, as at this very moment, I was perceived by them. I sprung forth from my hiding place, and succeeded in out-running them for some time; but becoming exhausted, I was caught by a strong Indian who raised his tomahawk to kill me, should I attempt to advance a step further. He demanded my surrender, and seeing no alternative, I gave up myself. I was immediately pinioned, and led a short distance from the house, to take a last look of my companion's mangled body. In a few minutes my surviving children were brought to the same spot, where we were compelled to remain without the liberty of speaking to each other, until these blood-thirsty wretches had packed up what they wished of my effects that had not been consumed. Having succeeded to their satisfaction, not only in destroying the lives of a few unoffending persons, but in totally destroying my property—which was the fruits of many a year's hard labor—they took up their line of march toward the northwest, compelling myself and children to accompany them.—They travelled with a good deal of speed, until they had reached a distance of 18 miles—and the reason of taking us here was soon made known—it was to consult together to see in what manner they should put my children to death!—The mode finally agreed upon, was, to *burn them alive!* Preparations were now made for the burning of one of them, and the rest saved for another time. A stake about 14 feet long was driven into the ground, to which my daughter was bound; and some dry brush was next gathered and piled around her to the height of her waist, which was set on fire, and burned, while they danced round the post, alternately breaking forth in songs of revelry, and uttering terrific yells! None but a parent can imagine what were my feelings at this moment! For half an hour my ears were pained with the shrieks and groans of my dying daughter; while they, to increase my distress, said that we all were to share a similar fate. This was communicated to me by the savage, to whom I have alluded as being the instigator of this fatal and unprovoked attack on my innocent family; who, during the sufferings of my daughter, cast on me a fiend-like look, at the same time pointing to a wound on his head, which he said was inflicted by me.

My poor child had now ceased to breathe. Her soul had left its mortal tenement, and soared on high to an immortality "among the Saints in Light." Nor could I feel otherwise than thankful that her sufferings were at an end.

The Indians, after slightly covering with earth the portion of their victim that remained unconsumed—which was done to prevent their pursuers from tracing them—they extinguished their fires; and preparatory to marching, they bound upon my back a leathern pack, which contained a portion of the articles they had brought from my house. It was a heavy burden, but I was obliged to carry it without a murmur; and indeed, my mind was so affected with the scenes I had witnessed, and with the horrible anticipation of what the fate of myself, and remaining children would be, that extraneous influences had but little effect upon me.

A little before evening we overtook a party of Indians who had been to Middlefield, a place six miles distant to exchange furs and meat for whiskey. Although they probably in their intercourse with the whites expressed great friendship, yet their exultations were unbounded when they saw that we were prisoners, and to witness the miseries of myself and children. My captors were eager to exhibit their plunder, some of which they now exchanged for whiskey—of which they all drank so freely, as soon as to become intoxicated, and to such a degree as to be unable to proceed any further that night. I now thought this would be the most favorable opportunity I should have to attempt my escape. In order to make me secure, they had strongly bound me with a cord, and gave me a sleeping place between two large Indians.—My children, very unfortunately, were placed some distance from me, and in such a situation as to render it very perilous for me to try to effect their escape, should I be able to make my own. About midnight, believing the Indians who guarded me to be in a sound sleep, I crept upon my hands and knees four or five rods with as little noise as possible; when finding that I had not waked them, I arose upon my feet, and walked very lightly away from them, until I had reached a distance, which I thought beyond their hearing. I now severed the cord, by which I was bound, by sawing it across a stone; when I commenced running, and continued to do so until daybreak, by which time I became exhausted, and my strength failed, and I found it impossible to proceed any further without rest. Although I had reached, as I thought, a distance of 12 miles or more from my savage foes, yet I was not without my fears that I might have been early missed, and pursued by them. I therefore crept in between two rocks, which were covered with bushes, as the most secure place I could find. But the horror with which my mind was filled by the scenes I had witnessed, prevented my obtaining that repose which I so much needed; and what served to distract my feelings still more, was, that my remaining children were yet left in their hands. The thought of their wretched condition, and of what their feelings must be when they found themselves deserted by one who should have been to them a protector, filled my mind with such poignant grief that I almost resolved to go back, and suffer with them, or if we were not immediately killed, help them if possible to escape. I feared they would receive greater torment in consequence of my having absconded. But, I at last came to the conclusion that if I returned, it would be impossible to effect their liberation; and it certainly would have been madness for me to have ventured back, without a probability of accomplishing that object. As I now commenced walking at a slow pace, considering whether it was best to go back, or to hasten to the nearest white settlement, and obtain assistance, and then return and try to rescue my children—at the moment it seemed as if I could distinctly hear them calling to me to help them make their escape! Then would I stop, and resolve to return at all hazards—but something prevented me. Thus did I resolve and re-resolve, conclude to do one thing and, then another, without effecting anything for half a day; when the thought occurred to me that it was my duty to invoke the aid of God to direct me what to do and which way to go; resolving that after making this petition, I would go the way that my inclinations led me. I fell upon my knees and sent up a prayer to this effect; and had scarcely concluded, when I was started by the barking of a dog, and directly at the sight of an Indian, who was running with full speed towards me ! I now felt as if I was lost, not doubting but that he was sent in pursuit of me. When within a short distance of me, he to my astonishment, seized his dog by the mouth to prevent his making a noise, and then lay down upon the ground and directed me to do the same. I obeyed him. And we had not remained in this situation long before we heard the Indian pow-wow, and very soon afterwards their footsteps, as they passed by us, apparently in very great haste. At that moment my Indian friend —for such it now appeared that he was—lifted up his head a little, to see what course they were steering. As soon as they were fairly out of sight, he arose and beckoned me to follow. We took another route from that of our pursuers, and traveled on in an Indian trot four miles before we halted; when my friend perceiving that I suffered much from bodily pain and fatigue, and also from hunger, took out a cake made from broken corn, and gave a part of it it to me,

which relieved me very much, for many hours had passed since I had partaken of any kind of food.

As soon as our repast was finished, he gave me, in as intelligible a manner as his broken English could convey, an account of what had taken place among my foes since I made my escape. He said that they discovered I was gone about an hour before day-break. When this was known, they resolved to find me if possible, and should they succeed in again taking me prisoner, I was to be put to death in the most savage and painful manner. I was to be stripped entirely naked and bound down to a log, then covered with pitch, and fire communicated to it ; while they would dance round me and make hideous noises and yells in order to enhance my sufferings. And my children were to be there and witness my agonizing death, and know that a like torment awaited them. Accordingly a few went to work and collected pitch from pine trees, and made every thing ready to effect their diabolical designs ; while the rest of the party set out in pursuit of me, guided by the very dog I have before mentioned ; which very fortunately for me, was the property of the friendly Indian to whom I was indebted for my life. He did not belong to this party of Indians, nor had he participated with them in their barbarous acts against my family ; but he belonged to another tribe, and as he had received many favors at the hands of the whites, continued their friend, and was ever ready to do them service. It was his wish that I might escape, and to aid me in doing this, he prevailed on the rest to suffer him to precede them, by the pretence that he could better put his dog upon my track ; and while proceeding, he was so fortunate as to fall in with me, as above related, and thus save me from the worst of deaths.

After we were somewhat refreshed, I promised my Indian friend that I would reward him well if he would conduct me the shortest route to Waltersville, a place where I desired to go; which he agreed to do. We now journeyed in that direction, and after walking about two days, reached there in safety. I saw many of my old friends and acquaintances, who were deeply affected at a recital of the scenes through which I had passed, and to learn the fate of my unhappy family; and so great were their emotions, that many were anxious to pursue and wreak vengeance upon the savages, and if my children were alive, to rescue them. Accordingly, about fifteen of them, with myself, and the friendly Indian as our guide, armed ourselves and proceeded in search of them. At my earnest request the company consented to go by the way of my late abode, and where my family had been murdered, that I might have an opportunity to gratify my feelings in performing the last sad offices of duty that the living owe the dead,—*a respectable interment*. A few days after our departure, we arrived at the place where I had lived; and there we found the mangled bodies of my wife and children, lying apparently on the same spot that I had last seen them. We now enclosed them in coffins made of rough slabs which we hastily put together, and "laid them in their last bed," beneath that oak tree yonder. (Here the old man directed our sight to a large oak tree at a little distance.) After this was done, and I had dropped a tear of sorrow upon the graves of my companion and little ones, we proceeded on our way as hastily as possible, and soon reached the place where my little daughters had been sacrificed; and the preceding day we arrived upon the ground where, as appearances indicated, the savages had encamped the very night that I had made my escape from them. The log was there, to which they intended to bind me, and a large quantity of splinters; but, thank God, it was not ordered that I should drink the dregs of this bitter cup which had been given to my wife and children. We could not trace our foes

any farther; and not knowing in which direction they had gone, we concluded it advisable to return. Our Indian guide now expressed a desire to go to his home; and after we had rewarded his services to us by giving him the horse on which he had rode, together with many other presents, he took his leave of us with a solemn promise to do all in his power to trace these savages, and if possible set free my captive children, provided they had not been put to death. If they were living, I offered him a large reward to acquaint me with the fact at the earliest opportunity; which he promised to do.

Our company now returned to the village from which we had started; where I remained a welcome guest among my friends, until a treaty of peace had been permanently established with all of the frontier Indians. And as no more depredations from the Indians might be expected, I concluded to go and take up my abode at the place of my late residence where most of the remains of my family lay buried. There, though I could not again see my departed friends and mingle in their society and join in "sweet converse" with them, yet I could visit their graves and drop the silent tear of affection and sorrow, unseen by mortal eye; and as I had learned that my remaining children were put to death, which left me alone in the wide world, I resolved that it was far better to retire to this place, where earthly hope had departed, and memory could never sleep, and yield me up to muse "under the shade of melancholy's bough," believing that the God of the mourner would send "a healing balm for every wound" and visit my afflicted soul with heavenly consolation. My family had been exemplary christians, and I was permitted to hope that our souls would one day be re-united in love and blessedness in a celestial existence.

I now built this log hut, with my own hands; where, I think I can say, I have spent many years of frugal comfort and lived at peace with the world. As there is no other

3

habitation near this, I have lived quite secluded, but no more so than I desired. It was in accordance with my feelings to keep away from society, for my objects of love had gone from this world, and I now resolved to remain by myself and enjoy my rambles and excursions alone. I therefore have never sought the sympathy of my fellow creatures, nor often invited any to visit my humble cot. And this, my friends, is the first time since I have lived in this building, that I have related the unhappy history of a portion of my life.

And now my friends—for I can believe you none other— I have at your request, related most of the incidents that have occurred during the last few years of my life. And should you be led to inquire by what means I have been upheld through so great amount of extreme anguish and suffering— I reply, by often recurring to that blessed book, (pointing to a large Bible, covered only with paste-board, which showed the signs of age and use) and making it "the man of my counsel," and looking to it for that consolation which "the world cannot give or take away." It has cheered my drooping spirits when fast sinking beneath the burden of a heart overflowing with sorrow. It has led me to that fountain which is open for "sin and uncleanness," and bid me exercise humble repentance, and drink deep of that bliss which swallows up in immortality. This has been my guide and will ultimately, I trust lead me to "those green pastures and beside the still waters" where "everlasting spring abides, and never withering flowers."

My friends, I can see the hand of my merciful Benefactor in the afflictive dispensations with which he has visited me. It is said, that "whom he loveth, he chasteneth." I believe it is even so. Had I been permitted to live in the bosom of my family, surrounded by every worldly prosperity and allurement that my eyes and my desire coveted, probably my heart would never have been his, nor my affections placed upon him, who has said, "My son give me thine heart."

Yes, I should have refused allegiance to my Maker, and have been left to sport awhile with the joys of this vain world as my cheif portion ; and at last, when this mortal was called to put on immortality, I should have been destitute of that "treasure in heaven" which constitutes the eternal happiness of every saint—*the approbation of a merciful God.*

I feel willing to give up my friends, every idol and worldly pleasure, if it seems necessary in the sight of my heavenly Father, in order that I may be made subservient to his glory and fitted for his immediate presence. But thanks be to him that this is not required of his creatures. He does not wish us unhappy in *this* world, nor the next. If in his infinite wisdom he knows that some of his creatures require a more rigid discipline than others, before their stubborn will is broken and their hearts melted in love and submission to him, how grateful ought we to be that we are "counted worthy" to suffer affliction, sorrow, pain, or even death, that we may become the "heirs of God, and joint heirs with Christ, to an inheritance incorruptible, and undefiled, that fadeth not away."

I have reason to bless God that I am still permitted to live and praise his name on the earth. I once was young, but now am old. My locks are already whitened for the tomb, and what wait I for ? May I not soon expect to meet my departed family and friends around the throne of god, and to unite with them in praises to the Lamb, forever and ever ? Yes, I trust I may. But yet, I would feel thankful that my life is prolonged, in order that I may be better prepared for his coming.

I have chosen to retire from the world, from its gayety, its pleasure sand allurements, to this secluded spot. Here, free from anxious care and worldly pursuit, I have lived for many years, and sought as I humbly trust that "preparation" which is requisite to the forgiveness of sin and acceptance through

Christ. Though I have been visited with sore bereavements yet I would praise the Lord for all the worldly comfort I am permitted to enjoy. I have health and the various necessaries that are required to sustain the body. And it is not the least of my blessings that I am in my old age permitted the use of my limbs; for it is an inestimable privilege that I can walk over these beautiful grounds and contemplate and admire the works of nature. It always proves beneficial to me. It leads me to look from nature up to "nature's God" in wonder and praise. "The firmament declareth his handy work"—"the trees clap their hands," and all nature rejoices. Every thing conveys a pleasant and instructive lesson. I cannot visit any portion of this beautiful land without seeing opportunities for being instructed. I find

"Tongues in trees, books in the running brooks,
Sermons in stones—and good in every thing."

I should be extremely negligent and culpable did I not endeavor to benefit myself by all these beautiful and instructive lessons. I love the works of nature, and do often drink deep of their pure and healthy waters.

But my friends, I will tire you no longer with my own history, and thoughts. Perhaps I have been tedious and even discovered much egotism, in giving you the history of my last few years, and in describing so minutely my every day thought and feeling. If so, I beg to be excused, and trust that what I have stated may be imputed to none but good motives. It now only remains for me once more to direct you to the Bible, as the rule of action, the guide of your lives; and may it prove "a lamp to your feet, and a light to your path," and lead you to wash in the healing waters of Siloam, until your souls are purified and counted worthy to join in the general song of the redeemed of all nations and kindred—*worthy is the Lamb who was slain, to receive glory, honor and praise, forever and ever.*

A REMINISCENCE.

It was in the month of September, 1814, while an unnatural war was raging between two nations, that a British and an American officer were traveling in company in that part of Upper Canada which borders on Lake Ontario. The American had been bearer of despatches to the British, and was being conducted through his majesty's dominions on his way back. They had stopped to pass the night at a house near which was encamped a body of Indians. As the American officer was sitting alone, his companion having left the house for a short time, he was interrupted by the entrance of a tall, savage looking Indian, who having gazed on the officer for a momet, commenced a conversation.

'You're an American officer?'

'Yes.'

'Are you a prisoner?'

'No.'

The cold and repulsive manner in which these laconic answers were uttered, seemed by no means to please the forest chieftan, who drew himself up, and haughtily demanded:

'Do you know who I am Sir? I am Captain B———. I am son of old Col. R———. I command all these Indians.'

A moment's reflection convinced the American of the folly of exasperating this redoubtable personage. He rose, approached the chief, and extended his hand.

'I have heard of you before, Captain B———. I am happy to see you, and proud of your acquaintance.'

B—— returned his salutation, and again inquired if he was a prisoner.

'I am not, Sir.'

Observing that the officer had again seated himself by the window, he added : 'You had better not sit by that window : them Indians will shoot you.'

'They would certainly not attempt to injure a person whom they supposed to be a prisoner,—a man in their power, under the charge of a British officer.'

'What do they care for all that ! They'll kill a white man whenever they can get a fair chance.'

The officer removed his seat, and changed the subject ; but B—— interrupted him, and in the same abrupt tone as before, asked : 'Do you Americans ever give quarter to an Indian?'

'Certainly,—always,' was the answer.

'Well, you're an officer,—I don't like to dispute your word ; but excuse me, Sir, I don't believe it.'

'I assure you that it is so. All civilized nations, all white people, make it a rule to spare the prisoner who asks for quarter. It is a law which they dare not break.'

'So you all say,' replied the Indian, 'but I don't believe it, and I'll tell you why. When General Hull was going to invade Canada,—before Brock took him,—there at Detroit,—he sent out a long talk,—a proclamation, he called it,—in which he said that no white man, found fighting by the side of an Indian, should receive quarter. Well, Sir, if they kill the white man, what will they do with the Indian along side of him ? Tell me that ?'

'General Hull wished, I suppose, to discourage the employment of Indians by the British. He abhorred their mode of warfare, and did not wish to be embroiled with the red people. Besides, what General Hull did is no rule. His whole course was disapproved by the American people and government.'

'That is all very well,—but don't tell me,—I know General Hull made use of that expression,—and I know very well that if white people won't give quarter to each other, its a bad chance for the poor Indian to get it.'

The American attempted to argue the matter. The Indian chief replied with a vehemence, in which the vindictiveness natural to his race seemed to be blended with the excitement of intoxication, and to have overcome the reserve and dignity which is usually observable in the deportment of the Indian warrior.

'I have nothing to do with the British, they employ me, it is true—but I don't like them—I don't like any white people— and I have determined never to give quarter to an American,— if I do I'll be d———d !'

'Well, but Captain B——, let me put a case. Here are you and I, who have now become somewhat acquainted. If we should meet hereafter in battle, we might probably know each other. Suppose I should fall into your hands in the woods, should present my sword to you, and claim your mercy,—what would you do ?'

'I'll tell you what I'd do, Sir : I'd have your scalp. I like you very well : some of the American's are rascals,—but I think you are a tolerably clever fellow,—you seem to be a getleman,—but don't you calculate upon that, for if ever you were to fall into my hands, I'd have my tomahawk into your head, and your scalp off in half a minute !' As he said this, he suited the action to the word, gave a whoop, and flourished his right hand around the head of the officer, in imitation of the act which he would doubtless have taken great satisfaction in performing. At this moment the British officer returned, and the Indian soon left the room.

Early the next morning the two officers proceeded on their way, and were enabled to reach their place of destination in safety.

The fierce and vicious savage, a part of whose conduct we have faintly described, was the son of a chief. The son was reared among the whites, and received a good English education; but returned to the savage life with a mind embittered against the whole white race, from whom he declared he had learned nothing, but to drink and swear,—accomplishments which, it must be allowed, he had attained to a disgusting perfection.

The character and fate of this Indian affords a strong evidence of the folly of attempting to civilize the savage, by extending to him the advantages of education, while all the temptations to resume his original mode of life are left strewed in his path. That the intelect of the Indian may be cultivated, there is no question: but of what avail are all efforts bestowed upon the culture of his mind, if his savage propensities remain unchanged, and the heart, fatally bent on mischief, is allowed to return to its first love.

Appendix 3

Facsimile of an "Official" Document – The Isaac Zane Deposition

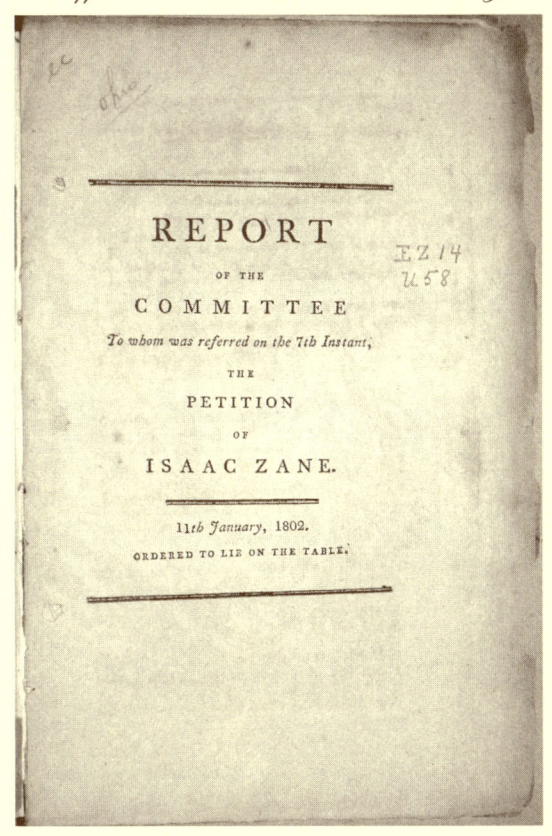

REPORT

OF THE

COMMITTEE

To whom was referred on the 7th Instant,

THE

PETITION

OF

ISAAC ZANE.

11th *January*, 1802.

ORDERED TO LIE ON THE TABLE.

REPORT.

The Committee to whom the Petition of ISAAC ZANE *was referred on the 7th instant, have taken the same into consideration, and make thereon the following*

REPORT:—

THAT the petitioner states, that he was made a prisoner by the Wyandot Indians when an infant of nine years of age, with which nation he has ever since remained, having married an Indian woman, by whom he has had many children: That his attachments to the whites has subjected him to numberless inconveniencies and dangers during the almost continual wars which existed between the United States and the Indians, until the peace of Greenville, in 1795:—That previous to that period, a tract of land, on which he now lives, had been assigned to him by the Wyandot Indians, and that no idea was entertained when that treaty was made, that the land which had been given him would fall within the boundary of the United States, (which now appears to be the case) and of consequence, no provision was made in his favor by the treaty; all of which the committee have reason to believe is perfectly true:—And it further appears from two certificates, one given by five Indian Chiefs, at a place called the Big Rock, on the sixteenth day of September, 1800:—That the Wyandot nation of Indians allotted the said Zane a tract of land, of four miles square, on Mad River, and that the said Zane had a pre-emption right,

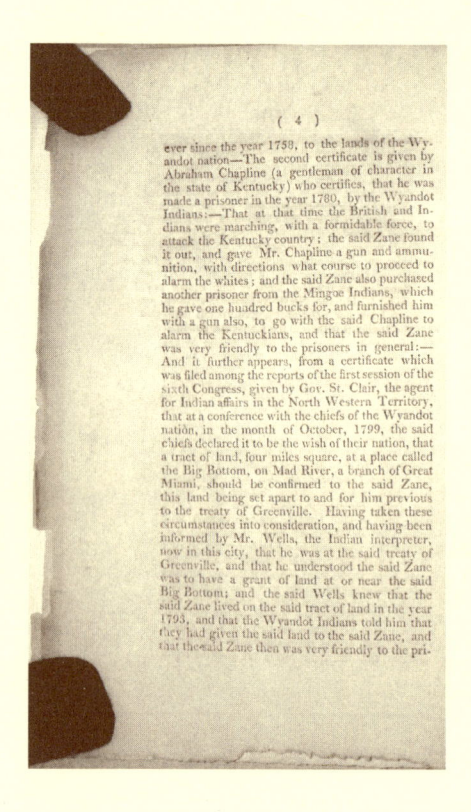

(4)

ever since the year 1759, to the lands of the Wyandot nation—The second certificate is given by Abraham Chapline (a gentleman of character in the state of Kentucky) who certifies, that he was made a prisoner in the year 1780, by the Wyandot Indians:—That at that time the British and Indians were marching, with a formidable force, to attack the Kentucky country; the said Zane found it out, and gave Mr. Chapline a gun and ammunition, with directions what course to proceed to alarm the whites; and the said Zane also purchased another prisoner from the Mingoe Indians, which he gave one hundred bucks for, and furnished him with a gun also, to go with the said Chapline to alarm the Kentuckians, and that the said Zane was very friendly to the prisoners in general:—And it further appears, from a certificate which was filed among the reports of the first session of the sixth Congress, given by Gov. St. Clair, the agent for Indian affairs in the North Western Territory, that at a conference with the chiefs of the Wyandot nation, in the month of October, 1799, the said chiefs declared it to be the wish of their nation, that a tract of land, four miles square, at a place called the Big Bottom, on Mad River, a branch of Great Miami, should be confirmed to the said Zane, this land being set apart to and for him previous to the treaty of Greenville. Having taken these circumstances into consideration, and having been informed by Mr. Wells, the Indian interpreter, now in this city, that he was at the said treaty of Greenville, and that he understood the said Zane was to have a grant of land at or near the said Big Bottom; and the said Wells knew that the said Zane lived on the said tract of land in the year 1795, and that the Wyandot Indians told him that they had given the said land to the said Zane, and that the said Zane then was very friendly to the pri-

(5)

soners that were taken by the Indians into captivity. Therefore the committee have considered that the petitioner ought to have confirmed a tract of land, equal in some degree to the intentions of the Indians, and to the services rendered to the United States by the petitioner; they therefore recommend to the House the adoption of the following resolution:—

Resolved, That a committee be appointed to bring in a bill authorising the President of the United States to convey, in fee simple, to Isaac Zane, six sections of land, of one square mile each, within the North Western Territory, on any lands not heretofore appropriated, and that the Indian title thereto has been extinguished.

(6)

WE, the Wyandot nation, having given to Isaac Zane a lot of land, consisting of four miles square, on the heads of Mad River, these five years past, and seems at present to encroach on the American lands; in that case we, the said Wyandot nation, allow the American government to take possession of as much land of theirs, to replace the said land given to the said Isaac Zane, although, at same time, the said Isaac Zane has had a pre-emption right since the year 1758.

Signed at the Big Rock, this sixteenth day of September, in the year of our Lord one thousand eight hundred.

Marks. { SAS TA RED ZI, SA EN TES CON, DES CHA RA MAN, SY ET TA, DA RI ON.

Signed in the presence of

Jas. Melvin,
Adam Brown,
William Walkaer,
J. B. P. Beaugrand,
James M'Reid.

I DO certify, That in the spring 1780, I was a prisoner with the Wyandot Indians, and that the British and Indians were marching to attack the Kentucky country with a formidable force, and Isaac Zane furnished me with a gun and ammunition, with instructions what course to proceed to alarm the people in Kentucky; and that he was very friendly to the prisoners in general, and certified to me his friendship to his native country-

(7)

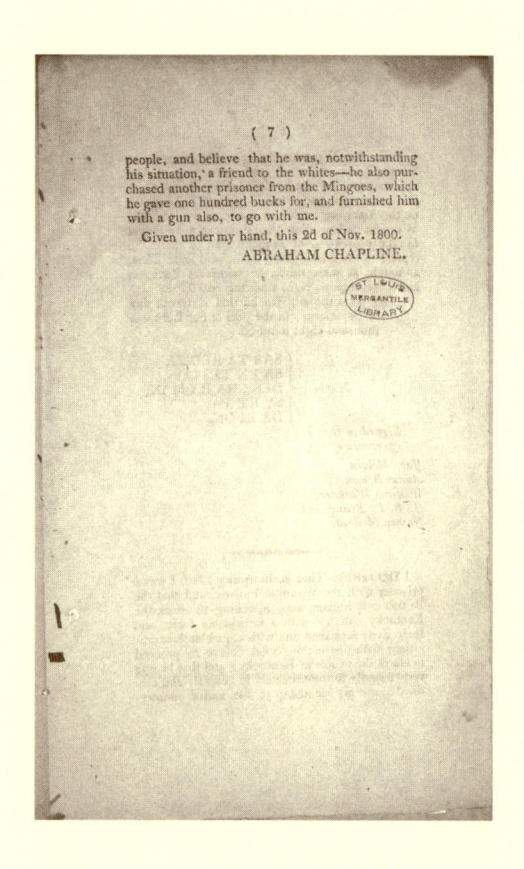

people, and believe that he was, notwithstanding his situation, a friend to the whites—he also purchased another prisoner from the Mingoes, which he gave one hundred bucks for, and furnished him with a gun also, to go with me.

Given under my hand, this 2d of Nov. 1800.

ABRAHAM CHAPLINE.

Adventures and Sufferings

ADVENTURES AND SUFFERINGS

Appendix 4:

Captive	Other Correspondents	Place
	R. J. Meigs	Fall of Ft. Dearborn
	Lt. Baker	Frenchtown Massacre
"Mrs. Helm"		Massacre of Ft. Dearborn
		Raisin River Massacre
Daniel Boone		
	Walter Jordan	Massacre at Chiago
Dr. Samuel McKeehan		Raisin River Massacre
"A Captive" (related to John Taylor)	Gov. Cass	Red River near Lake Winepee
"A Frenchman"		On the Missouri River
White Persons among the Indians	Gov. Lewis Cass	
"Lt. Adams"		
"General Ashley"		Rocky Mts.
"traders"		
Pawnee village massacre		
"Hall Sisters"	*Rock Spring Baptist*	Illinois
	St. Louis Beacon	
"Captain Ford and a company of rangers"	*Louisville Herald*	
"Santa Fe Traders"		Canadian fork of the
"Blackfeet hostages"	*Buffalo Republican*	Arkansas River
Gabriel Martin	Colonel Dodge	
"Two American Boys"	*Little Rock Gazette*	Texas
"William Cooley, his wife	"A St. Augustine Letter"	Florida
three daughters and a hired teacher"	400 black slaves	
"General Clinch"	*Savannah Georgian*	Florida (Wythlacooche River)
"Six People Killed"	"Chief Tabaquina"	Coffee's Trading Post
	"General Coffee"	
"150 people massacred"	*Charlestown Courier*	Indian Key
Mrs. Montgomery and her escort	*Charlestown Courier*	Micanopy Area
"A Spanish woman and a young girl"	R.A. Calloway	
"General Buleson"		Linnville, Texas
"a White Captive"	E. A. Hitchcock	
	J. C. Spencer	
Sister of Mr. Slocum	Wilkes Barre Advocate	Pennsylvania

*From an unpublished paper by David Reiter, "The Search for Indian Captivities in *The Weekly Register*"

Captivity Accounts Reported in *Niles' Weekly Register**

Tribes	Date of Account	Published in Niles
	9/1/1812	Sept., 1812 (v-3 p.79)
	1/22/1813	March 27, 1813 (v-4, pp. 67-68)
	3/8/1813	April 3, 1813 (v-4, p. 82)
	2/14/1813	Oct. 23, 1813 (v-4, p. 92)
	2/7/1778	March 13, 1813 (v-4, pp. 34-35)
	10/19/1812	May 8, 1813 (v-4, p. 110)
	1/31/1813	June 12, 1913 (v-4, p. 244)
	about 1790	Sept. 19, 1818 (v.15, p.64)
Osage	n.d.	Sept. 20, 1823 (v-25, p. 39)
	1/7/1825	Mar. 19, 1813 (v.28, p.38)
Blackfeet	n.d.	Dec. 1, 1827 (v.33, p.213)
Iowa	1830	July 23, 1831 (v. 37, p.1)
Osage	5/29/1830	Aug. 31, 1830 (v.38, p458-9)
(Sauk)	June 1832	Oct. 27, 1832 (v.42, p.200 and v.43, p.132)
Comanche	2/19/1833	March 2, 1833 (v.44, p. 2,19)
Comanche	3/22/1833	March 23, 1833 (v.44, p.51)
	7/5/1833	July 20, 1833 (v.44, p.348)
Pawnee	9/13/1834	Sept. 20, 1834 (v.47, p.38)
Comanche	1/12/1836	Feb. 20, 1836 (v.49, p.425)
Seminole	12/22/1835	Jan. 9, 1836 (v. 69, p.313)
Seminole	12/30/1835	Jan. 30, 1836 (v. 49, p.369)
Pawnee	3/14/1836	April 16, 1836 (v. 50, p.121)
Seminole	8/7/1840	Sept. 5, 1840 (v.59, p.3)
	12/29/1839	"an. 16, 1840 (v.59, p. 307)
Comanche	10/2/1841	Oct. 2, 1841 (v. 61, p.66)
Comanche		June 4, 1842 (v. 62, P. 219)
Creek	1817-1818 (During the Cree, War)	May 13, 1843 (v. 64, p. 167)
	18th Century	[Obit]June 19, 1847 (v. 72, p. 243)

(St. Louis, University of Missouri – St. Louis, Dec. 2002 for History Class 403, Mercantile Library Seminar)

A Selected Bibliography

Baker, C. Alice
True Stories of New England Captives Carried to Canada During the Old French and Indian Wars.
Cambridge:Hall, 1897.

Bieder, Robert E.
Science Encounters the Indian, 1820-1880: The Early Years of American Ethnology.
Norman: The University of Oklahoma Press, 1986.

Blaisdell, Bob, ed.
Great Speeches by Native Americans.
New York: Dover, 2000.

Burnham, Michelle
Captivity and Sentiment: Cultural Exchange in American Literature, 1682-1861.
Hanover: Dartmouth and University Press of New England, 1997.

Calloway, Colin G.
North Country Captives; Selected Narratives of Indian Captivity from Vermont and New Hampshire.
Hanover: University Press of New England, 1992.

Castiglia, Christopher.
Bound and Determined; Captivity, Culture-Crossing, and White Womanhood from Mary Rowlandson to Patty Hearst.
Chicago: University of Chicago Press, 1996.

Child, Lydia Maria
Hobomok & Other Writings on Indians, edited by Carolyn L. Karcher.
New Brunswick, N.J.: Rutgers, 1986.

Coleman, Emma Lewis
New England Captives Carried to Canada Between 1677 and 1760 During the French and Indian Wars.
Portland, Maine: Southwark Press, 1925.

Demos, John
The Unredeemed Captive; A Family Story from Early America.
New York: Knopf, 1994.

Derounian-Stodola, Kathryn Z. ed.
Women's Indian Captivity Narratives.
New York: Penguin, 1998.

Derounian-Stodola, Kathryn Z. ed. & Levernier, J. ed.
The Indian Captivity Narrative, 1550-1900.
New York: Twayne, 1997.

Drimmer, Frederick, ed.
Captured by the Indians: 15 Firsthand Accounts, 1750-1870.
New York: Dover, 1985.
(originally published as *Scalps and Tomahawks: Narratives of Indian Captivity.*
New York: Coward-McCann, 1961.

Ewers, John C.
Not Quite Redmen. "The Plains Indian Illustrations of Felix O. C. Darley" *The American Art Journal,* Vol. 3, No. 2 (Fall, 1971)

Hoover, John Neal
"Scenes in Indian Life" and the Mid-Nineteenth Century Image of Native Americans
Mercantile Library Report to Members (2000-2001) pages 7-14.

Hunter, John Dunn
Memoirs of a Captivity Among the Indians of North America ed. by Richard Drinnon.
New York: Schocken Books, 1973.

Jaenen, Cornelius J.
Friend and Foe: Aspects of French-Amerindian Cultural Contact in the Sixteenth and Seventeenth Centuries.
New York: Columbia University Press, 1976.

Keiser, Albert
The Indian in American Literature.
New York: Oxford University Press, 1933.

Kennedy, J. H.
Jesuit and Savage in New France.
New Haven: Yale University Press, 1950.

Kephart, Horace, ed.
Captives Among the Indians: First-Hand Narratives of Indian Wars, Customs, Tortures, and Habits of Life in Colonial Times.
New York: Outing Publishing Co., 1915.

Kolodny, Annette.
The Land Before Her; Fantasy and Experience of the American Frontiers, 1630-1860.

Leach, Douglas Edward
Flintlock and Tomahawk: New England in King Philip's War.
New York: Norton, 1966.

Lepore, Jill
The Name of War; King Philip's War and the Origins of American Identity.
New York; Knopf, 1998.

Lincoln, Charles H., ed.
Narratives of the Indian Wars, 1675-1699.
New York: Scribners, 1913.

Miner, William Harvey
The American Indians North of Mexico.
Cambridge: University Press, 1917.

Miner, William Harvey
Daniel Boone: Contribution Toward a Bibliography of Writings Concerning Daniel Boone.
New York: Dibdin Club, 1901.

Miner, William Harvey, ed.
The Iowa: A Reprint from The Indian Record, as Originally Published and Edited by Thomas Foster.
Cedar Rapids, Iowa: Torch Press, 1911.

Namias, June
White Captives; Gender and Ethnicity on the American Frontier.
Chapel Hill: University of North Carolina, 1993.

Peckham, Howard H.
Captured by Indians: True Tales of Pioneer Survivors.
New Brunswick, N.J.: Rutgers University Press, 1954.

Peckham, Howard H.
Pontiac and the Indian Uprising.
Princeton, N.J.: Princeton University Press, 1947.

Plummer, Rachel
Rachael Plummer's Narrative of Twenty-One Months Servitude as a Prisoner Among the Commanchee Indians
with a preface by Archibald Hanna, and an introduction by William S. Reese.
Austin: Jenkins Publishing Co., 1977.

Rister, Carl Coke
Border Captives: The Traffic in Prisoners by Southern Plains Indians, 1835-1875.
Norman: University of Oklahoma Press, 1940.

Rister, Carl Coke

Comanche Bondage: Dr. John Charles Beale's Settlement of La Villa de Dolores on Las Moras Creek in Southern Texas of the 1830's, with an Annotated Reprint of Sarah Ann Horn's Narrative of Her Captivity Among the Comanches, Her Ransom by Traders in New Mexico, and Return via the Santa Fe Trail.
Glendale, Calif.: Arthur H. Clark, 1955.

Rosenbach Museum & Library

Carried Away by Indians: Indian Captivity Narratives and the Evolution of a Stereotype
catalogue for an exhibition 17 Jan.-28 Apr., 1985, organized and curated by Leslie A. Morris and Ridie E. W. Ghezzi.

Seaver, James Everett

A Narrative of the Life of Mary Jemison, the White Woman of the Genesee
revised by Charles Delamater Vail
New York: American Scenic & Historic Preservation Society, 1918.
A modern edition by June Namias is available from the University of Oklahoma Press, Norman, 1992.

Smith, DeCost

Indian Experiences.
Caldwell, Idaho: Caxton Printers, 1943.

Tebbel, John

The Compact History of the Indian Wars.
New York: Hawthorn Books, 1966.

Rowson, Susanna.

Charlotte Temple.
New York: Oxford University Press, 1986.

Utley, Robert M.
The American Heritage History of the Indian Wars
with Wilcomb E. Washburn, ed. by Anne Moffat and Richard F. Snow
New York: American Heritage, 1977.

Vail, R. W. G.
The Voice of the Old Frontier.
Philadelphia: University of Pa., 1949.

Vaughan, Alden T.
Narratives of North American Indian Captivity: A Selective Bibliography.
New York: Garland, 1983.

Vaughan, Alden T.
New England Frontier: Puritans and Indians, 1620-1675.
Boston: Little, Brown, 1965.

Vaughan, Alden T. and Clark, Edward W. editors.
Puritans Among the Indians; Accounts of Captivity and Redemption, 1676-1724.
Cambridge: Belknap-Harvard, 1981.

Vaughan, Alden T. and Richter, Daniel K.
Crossing the Cultural Divide: Indians and New Englanders, 1605-1763.
Worcester: American Antiquarian Society, 1980.

VanDerBeets, Richard
The Indian Captivity Narrative: An American Genre.
Lanham, MD: University Press of America, 1984.

Index of Key Names with Associated Items

Aa, Pieter vander; 115
Alexander, J.H.; 41
Austin, Stephen; 5 B

Babb, Theodore A.; 15
Baldwin, Elmer; 13
Baldwin, Thomas; 22
Barber, Mary; 7
Bard, Catharine Poe; 42
Bard, Richard; 42
Barnwell, Ella; 121
Bartlett, Joseph; 148
Beatty, Charles; 36
Belden, George P.; 96
Belknap, Jeremy; 141
Bennett, Emerson; 121;,126
Berghold, Alexander; 62
Biggs, William; 67
Bird, Robert Montgomery; 122
Black Hawk; 13, 76
Blake, Alexander V.; 90
Bogart, W.H.; 20
Boone, Daniel; 16, 20, 119
Bosman, Richard; 54
Brayton, Matthew; 43
Bressani, Francesco Giuseppe; 40
Brigdon, Philip; 13
Brisbin, James; 96
Brownell, Charles de Wolf; 99

Bryant, Charles S.; 33

Cabeza de Vaca, Alvar Nuñez; 53
Carrigan, Minnie Buce; 49
Carter, E.S.; 30
Cass, Lewis; 5
Catlin, George; 5
Caverly, Robert; 54
Charlevoix, P.F.X. de; 85
Chouteau, Pierre; 5
Clark, William; 5
Colden, Cadwallader; 74
Coleson, Annie; 8
Cook, Darius B.; 50
Corbly, John; 3
Cornelius, Elias; 19
Corwin, Hugh D.; 149
Cutler, Jervis; 123

DeForest, John W.; 97
DeShields, James T.; 29
Dodge, J.R.; 75
Dolbeare, Benjamin; 120
Drake, Benjamin; 76, 77
Drake, Samuel G.; 27, 33, 35, 109
Drinnon,Richard; 5
Duston, Hannah; 27, 54

Eastburn, Joseph; 136

Eastburn, Robert; 5, 136
Eastman, Edwin; 15
Eastman, Mary H.; 103, 104
Eastman, Seth; 88
Edwardsville Spectator; 114
Ellis, Edward S.; 145

Filson, John; 20
Finley, James B.; 64
Flint, Timothy; 20
Fulton, A.R.; 100

Gardiner, Abigail; 18
Gay, Bunker; 141
Gilbert, Benjamin; 46, 137
Giles, John; 44
Goodrich, Samuel G.; 93
Grey Hawk; 80

Hall, Almira
  (Sylvia Hall or Mrs. Horn); 13
Hall, Frances
  (Rachel Hall or Mrs. Munson); 13
Hall, J.W.; 13
Hall, James; 84
Hallberger, Eduard; 20
Harbison (or Herbeson),
  Massey (or Massy); 3, 10
Harris, Caroline; 1
Hartley, Cecil; 146
Hawthorne, Nathaniel; 54
Heard, Isaac V.D.; 125

Heartman, Charles; 67
Heckewelder, John; 110
Horn, Sarah Ann; 14
House, E.; 14
How, Nehemiah; 59
Howe, Henry; 144
Howe, Jemima; 141
Hoyt, Elihu; 132
Hoyt, Jonathan; 132
Hubbard, John Niles; 143
Hubbard, William; 35
Humfreville, J. Lee; 101
Hunter, John D.; 5

Illinois Historical Library; 67

Jaenen, Cornelius; 40
James, Edwin; 37
Jefferys, Thomas; 34
Jemison, Mary; 51
Jenkins, John S.; 20
Jewitt, John; 56
Johnson, Susannah Willard; 25
Johnston, Charles; 47
Johonnot, Jackson; 3, 10, 11
Jones, Daniel W.; 102
Jones, J.B.; 116, 127
Jones, U.J.; 52

Keim, De Benneville Randolph; 98
Kelly, Fanny; 61
Kephart, Horace; 5, 11, 40

King Philip; 27, 35
Knight, John; 26
Knox, John; 87

Lahontan, Baron Louis-Armand; 38
Lee, L.P.; 18
Lee, Nelson; 21
Lehmann, Herman; 63
Leith, John; 57
Le Raye, Chas.; 123
Lewis, Hannah; 12
Lewis, James O.; 113
Livingston, William; 106
Long, John; 89
Loomis, Augustus Ward; 92
Loskiel, George Henry; 112

Macaulay, James; 80
Maso, Augustus Lynch; 117
M'Conkey, Harriet E. Bishop; 33
McIntosh, John; 108
McKenney, Thomas L.; 84
McLean, John; 82
McMechen, James H.; 139
Manheim, Frederic; 3
Marrant, John; 9
Mather, Cotton; 27, 35, 54
Mather, Increase; 27
M'Gaw, James F.; 124
Meginness, John F.; 48
Menzies, David; 31

Meredith, Grace E.; 142
Metcalf, Samuel L.; 16
Milet, Peter; 45
Miner W.H.; 115
Mogridge, George; 91
Murch, Abel B.; 33
Myrtle, Minnie
  (Anna C. Miller); 95

Newson, T.M.; 68
Northrup, Henry Davenport; 118
Norton, Frank H.; 119

"Oatman girls"; 23
O'Connell, Alexander; 114
Ogden, David; 24
Ogden, Peter; 69
Oswego; 106

Parker, Cynthia Ann; 29
Parker, Quanah; 29
Patterson, A.W.; 73
Paul, James; 2
Peck, John Mason; 38, 40, 114
Penhallow, Samuel; 27
Persinger, Joseph; 17
Pettijohn, Jonas; 32
Plummer, Clarissa; 1, 29
Plummer, Rachel; 29
Pote, William; 70
Pouchot, Pierre; 86
Priest, Josiah; 24, 134

Adventures and Sufferings

Pritts, Joseph; 78

Reese, William; 29
Reynolds, John; 13, 52
Riggs, G. W.; 53
Riggs, Stephen R.; 66
Robb, John S.; 128
Ronan, Peter; 72
Ross, L.S.; 29
Rowlandson, Mary; 55
Rowson, Susannah; 138

St. Clair, General Arthur; 10, 11, 16
St. Louis Lyceum Library; 56
Scanlan, Charles M.; 13
Schoolcraft, Henry Rowe; 88, 107
Scott, Hervey; 52
Seaver, James E.; 51
Seymour, Philip; 124
Shafford, John C.; 140
Shea, John Gilmary; 81
Sherrard, Robert A.; 2
Slocum, Frances; 48
Slover, John; 26
Smith, Elbert H.; 76
Smith, James; 75
Smith, John; 115
Smith, Mary; 133
Spencer, O.M.; 4
Squatting Bear; 7
Squier, E.G.; 38, 53

Steele, Zadock; 71
Stewart, Isaac; 3
Stinnett, Albert Sidney; 15
Stratton, R.B.; 23
Swanton, Hannah; 135
Sylvester, George Henry; 131
Sylvester, Herbert Milton; 83

Tanner, John; 37
Taylor, James B.; 6
Tecumseh; 50, 77
Thomson, Charles; 36
Thoreau, Henry David; 54
Timberlake, Henry; 39
Triplett, Frank; 105
Turner, Chipman; 52
Turner, George; 94
Tuttle, C.R.; 111

Walton, William; 46
Webster, Dolly; 120
Webster, John; 120
Wetmore, Alphonso; 79
Wetzel, Lewis; 146
White, Henry; 147
Whittier, John Greenleaf; 54
Wilkinson, Peter; 3
Williams, John; 60; 132
Williams, Stephen; 60
Williamson, Peter; 28

Zane, Isaac; 130

ADVENTURES AND SUFFERINGS

This catalogue was prepared, in conjunction with an exhibition, by John Neal Hoover, Executive Director, St. Louis Mercantile Library at the University of Missouri – St. Louis.

500 copies of this catalogue were designed and printed by Chelmsford Printing, Inc. of St. Louis, Missouri on 80# Natural Sundance Text and 80# Rawhide Sundance Cover. It was electronically set using Embassy Script, Times Roman, Memphis (electronically condensed), and Old English. Typesetting was by Adrian Creative Services, Inc.